The Visibility Trap

The Visibility Trap

Sexism, Surveillance and Social Media

Mary McGill

NEW ISLAND

THE VISIBILITY TRAP
First published in 2021 by
New Island Books
Glenshesk House
10 Richview Office Park
Clonskeagh
Dublin D14 V8C4
Republic of Ireland
www.newisland.ie

Print ISBN: 978-1-84840-801-2
eBook ISBN: 978-1-84840-802-9

British Library Cataloguing in Publication Data. A CIP catalogue record for this book is available from the British Library.

Typeset by JVR Creative India
Edited by Djinn von Noorden
Cover design by Jack Smyth, jacksmyth.co
Cover photograph shows a basalt statue of Aphrodite (late 1st–early 2nd century A.D.), held in The MET Museum, New York; rawpixel #2554808.
Index by Jane Rogers
Printed by FINIDR, s.r.o., Czech Republic, finidr.com

New Island Books is a member of Publishing Ireland.

10 9 8 7 6 5 4 3 2 1

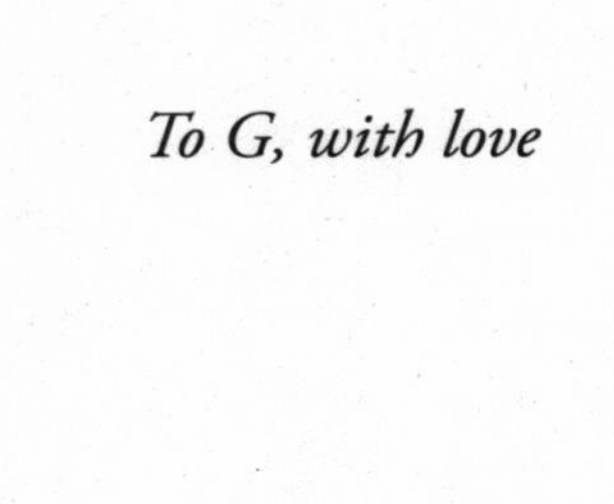

To G, with love

Contents

Introduction

In mid-2020, in the first of many waves of the virus, I realised we were living through not one pandemic but two.

Standing by my kitchen radio one June lunchtime I listened as a young woman named Róisín told Joe Duffy about her experience of image-based abuse[1] when, aged just seventeen, she was filmed by her classmates having sex while intoxicated on a night out, without her knowledge. 'It was one of the worst moments of my life,' she said, describing how she felt the next day when she discovered the video was being shared on social media.[2] Despite her ordeal and the risk of further public shaming, Róisín braved national radio to make an important point about the abuse she endured. 'Parents and teachers, they don't realise how common it is,' she explained, adding that those who filmed her 'probably still don't understand the consequences.'[3]

As a society, Ireland had been here before. Back in 2013 the infamous 'Slane Girl' case saw images of a teenage girl engaged in an intimate act with a guy, taken at an Eminem concert at Slane Castle, go viral. The pictures were shared thousands of times across platforms like Facebook, Instagram and Twitter in Ireland and further afield, before being removed when it came to light that the girl was under eighteen.[4] By then, the damage was more than done. The victim had been hospitalised. The international media had weighed in. The internet was aflame with opprobrium. About society's response, the novelist Lisa McInerney made a salient remark: 'As the moral authority of the Church wanes, a new religion takes its place. Its methods might be different, but that's just new perfume applied to the same old shit. Trial by social media: it's quick, it's brutal, and it's very, very disappointing.'[5]

In the Slane Girl case, severe judgement was heaped upon the victim who was called, amongst other things, a 'vile slut'.[6] By comparison, the young man involved was proclaimed a 'hero'.[7] Róisín described the same double standard: while she was shamed and ostracised, her partner was a declared a 'legend'.[8] In both cases, the rush to victim-blame left little space for reflecting on the ethics of sharing such material or questioning of why it was allowed to circulate with such impunity, despite the obvious harm it was causing. Although the technology on which these events played out was new, the attitudes involved were not: they were rooted in a centuries-old distrust of female sexuality and a cultural predilection for making a spectator sport out of blaming women.

Seven years after Slane Girl, listening to Róisín, it was clear to me that things had not got better. In fact, they appeared to be getting worse. In the summer of 2020 Ireland still lacked fit-for-purpose laws to deal with image-based abuse.[9] Meanwhile, the sudden shift to online living from March 2020 seemed to be feeding some of the worst aspects of human behaviour, among them misogyny and the desire to humiliate. While profit projections for social media companies soared as our screens become even more indispensable, so too did levels of gender-based digital abuse. This reflected trends already well established long before Covid-19. Our 'new normal' was now intensifying them, with devastating consequences.

As a digital-culture researcher and journalist,[10] I realised that Róisín's story, although specific to Ireland, resonated far beyond. It captured a phenomenon that, like all viruses, has local and global dimensions and is highly mobile and adaptive. It stems from a world where, as surveillance-studies professor David Lyon writes, watching and being watched, often through the prism of technology, has become a part of everyday life.[11] This new visibility has its pleasures and benefits but it also heralds multiple problems that we are only now beginning to name and understand. It speaks to a moment in Western culture that has been building for over a decade, where our once-enthusiastic embrace of digital technology is shifting as the downsides become too uncomfortable to ignore. For women and girls, these downsides can have life-changing consequences, turbo-charging old foes such as sexism and beauty pressures while gifting abusers new, highly destructive tools.

This new visibility has an impact on both private citizens like Róisín and those in the public eye. In October 2020 the National University of Ireland, Galway, released findings as part of an ongoing study into online abuse and threats of violence against women politicians.[12] Based on interviews with sixty-nine current and former members of government and female councillors from all the major political parties, it found that 96 per cent of interviewees 'have received social media or email messages that used threatening language or "hate mail", while three-quarters say they have been threatened with physical violence via online or social media'.[13] One interviewee, a former TD, told the researchers: 'I was repeatedly threatened by a troll who threatened to throw acid in my face. Another once said he knew where I lived and he'd be standing in my garden waiting for me.'[14] The research said that while a 'small minority' of interviewees reported the abuse to authorities, including social media companies, they got the sense that it wasn't taken seriously given 'a perception that politicians were "fair game"'.[15]

High-profile women in Irish sport are also singled out for this type of abuse.[16] In November 2020 TG4 announced its first all-female panel for the broadcast of Leinster's game against Cardiff in the rugby Pro14. What should have been a landmark moment for women in sports broadcasting in this country was met with a deluge of online negativity.[17] And it's not just what happens around games, but off the pitch too. In February 2021 the broadcaster and former Irish basketball player Emer O'Neill told Newstalk radio about the sexist and racist abuse she experienced online. O'Neill, who is of Irish and Nigerian descent, called social media 'a free-for-all', describing the horrible comments left on an image she posted to Instagram of her breastfeeding her infant daughter: 'I'm trying to normalise breastfeeding, it's a beautiful thing, I don't think women should be ashamed of it, and I think it's something that should be out there, it's important to me. Underneath this beautiful picture of a mother nourishing her child, a man wrote "Ugly Blackie".'[18]

Incidents of image-based abuse and threats to women in the public eye are just some examples of the immense power that digital technology, especially social media, now has over so many aspects of our lives, including the most private. This power shapes how we interact with our friends, family and partners, how we build our careers, express our politics, find love, have fun, get our information and perhaps most fundamentally, how we feel about ourselves. Their impact should not be underestimated. As critic John R. Culkin observed, referring to the work of media theorist Marshall McLuhan on the nature of technology, 'We shape our tools and thereafter they shape us.'[19]

Social media has become mainstreamed into our lives so quickly it has outpaced our ability to set boundaries, to create the space to reflect, to opt out. This book is an attempt to readjust that balance. It explores some of the many ambiguities of what it means for women to live in a social media-made world, among technologies that are sold as liberating and 'empowering' despite ample evidence to the contrary. As communications professor Sarah Banet-Weiser writes, this empowerment-through-visibility 'is often achieved through a focus on the visible body – precisely one of the aspects of patriarchy feminism has been fighting against for centuries'.[20] In this landscape of contradictions, 'the visibility trap' is a way of understanding how the demands of online visibility are shaping women's self-representations, and what this means for the individual and for equality. This book explores how the trap works and how we might be more mindful of it – a process that begins with building a critical awareness about the downsides of visibility as much as its positives. As virtual-reality pioneer Jaron Lanier writes on how to build better relationships with social media and indeed better social platforms in general, 'Awareness is the first step to freedom.'[21]

We begin by exploring how women's online visibility today is still subject to the same cultural constraints that have long sought to control their entry to the public sphere.

After that, we look at selfies and the fragmented self, and the tensions that arise between our digital self-image and our embodied selves. Then we turn to Instagram and the ways new forms of visibility are used to determine who gets to be seen and who doesn't, and what this means for representation and bodies outside the norm. Next, we explore harmful aspects of the influencer industry, exemplified by the Kardashian Industrial Complex (KIC) that uses a repackaged beauty myth and the allure of hyper-visibility to sell compelling but elusive versions of 'the good life' to a vast female consumer base. After that, from dating apps to image-based abuse, we look at how the visibility, surveillance and access enabled by the internet in the digital age has contributed to new forms of harassment and a resurgence of misogyny. Finally, we consider the changemakers – the activists and thinkers holding social media companies to account, reimagining how our relationship to this technology could look if digital platforms supported equality rather than threatened it.

Welcome to the world of the visibility trap. Please, mind your step.

One

Let's Get Visible

'There is power in looking.'
bell hooks[1]

How many selfies does it take to ruin a life? If you are a woman, just one will do.

When 25-year-old New York maths teacher Lauren Miranda was called to a meeting in her principal's office in January 2019, little did she know that the career she had worked so hard for was about to be snatched away. A colleague had earlier warned Miranda of a rumour circulating, which suggested that a student had somehow got hold of a topless selfie of her. Confident that this could not be true, Miranda found herself at the meeting with the principal and other school-board members, most of whom were male. According to Miranda, the principal asked her, 'Do you take pictures?' before spinning around his computer screen to show her topless selfie.[2] In an instant, Miranda's life as she had known it was over, destroyed by a single image taken years before that she had forgotten existed. Describing her horror at being confronted in this way, Miranda recalled shaking with distress and a deep sense of violation, later telling a reporter, 'I'd never felt so small before.'[3] On the drive home afterwards, she had to pull over to vomit.

Miranda's punishment did not stop there. Claiming that she was no longer 'role model' material, the school district first suspended, then fired her.[4] The story might have ended at this point were it not for Miranda's refusal to be shamed for an image she described as 'pure'; an image she said she had taken and sent to a former boyfriend years before, who was at the time a teacher in the same school district.[5] How the selfie ended up in the hands of a student was unclear. Nevertheless, according to Miranda, a school-district superintendent told her that he pitied her, asking, 'How can I put you in front of a classroom full of boys where they can pull out their phones and look at this image of you?'[6] As far as those in power seemed to be concerned, it was less about how Miranda's image came to be circulated without her knowledge or consent, representing a gross invasion of her privacy, and more about judging her for taking the image in the first place.

Given the severity of her treatment, no one would have blamed Miranda for withdrawing from the controversy, but she chose to fight. 'Men and women are equal,' she said flatly when asked about her decision to sue the school board for $3 million. 'It's 2019. My chest is no more offensive than a man's chest so why am I being penalised? If a man took the same picture, he wouldn't be in the same situation I'm in.'[7] In a statement to *Buzzfeed News*, Miranda pointed out the hypocrisy at play, arguing that men sexualise women's bodies whether they want them to or not: 'They really blame women for being women. They make us out to be sexual deviants, instead of seeing us as appreciating the beauty of ourselves.'[8] In another interview, this time with *VICE News*, Miranda outlined how her stance speaks to a much larger issue that girls and women now have to navigate; where the circulation of images enabled by social media makes them vulnerable to being watched, shamed and judged in ways unimaginable just a generation ago. 'How do girls feel when this happens to them?' she asks. 'Their photo gets shared without their permission or consent and what do we say to them? Crawl in a hole? Quit going to school? Go to private school, get home-schooled? What do I say when those girls have to go back to their classrooms and, you know, interact with their peers?'[9]

When Miranda's story first broke I was in the final stages of a writing a doctoral study on the selfie phenomenon, exploring how the intensely visual cultures of social media are shaping the way women are seen and see themselves in contemporary societies. Using what is known in scholarly fields such as media studies and cultural studies as an 'audience studies' approach, I wanted to gain deeper insight into how these technologies were interpreted and used in everyday life by a cohort regarded as their most enthusiastic proponents: young women. Miranda's experience mirrored many of the themes I had encountered in my work, themes that reflect a digital world rife with contradictory expectations. On the one hand, she was using this powerful, still relatively new technology to enjoy her femininity, to represent herself as she desired, and to share this pleasure with someone of her choosing. On the other, that same technology, drawing on a long history of punishing women for their sexuality, was used to humiliate and disgrace her by enabling her image to be circulated in ways she could not foresee and did not consent to.

This shaming was not restricted to the internet. Far from it. It produced very real problems for Miranda's professional and personal life, indicating how immaterial the dichotomy between 'offline' and 'online' has become. Yet what Miranda did, in taking a 'sexy' selfie, was hardly remarkable. In the age of the smartphone (and a pandemic that has made physical intimacy difficult, especially for single people) sexting and sending nudes are modern courtship rituals many people engage in, which prompts the question – how many potential cases like Lauren Miranda's are there out there?

Given that tens of millions of selfies are uploaded every day, thousands upon thousands seems like a conservative guess. But bear in mind, too, that technology has progressed to such an extent that the simple selfie is, in some respects, the least of it. Easily available AI can now generate deepfake imagery and videos of celebrities and private individuals, producing results that are startling for their realness.[10] In the digital age, images of women have never been so plentiful, and never so potentially destructive.

Miranda's story – and many more like it, few of which receive the same level of attention – serve as a reminder of how heavily attitudes to women's use of new technologies and their presence on social media platforms are shaped by archaic notions of purity, deviancy and 'correct' feminine behaviour. As Miranda points out, women's bodies are sexualised whether or not they want them to be, often in a manner that cannot accommodate the idea that a woman enjoying her own image is anything other than a narcissistic harlot. Even when a grown woman creates an image of herself for her pleasure and decides to share it with someone of her choosing, some cannot help but cast this agency as aberrant. By electing to engage in what is depicted as 'risky' sexual behaviour, the fault is positioned at the feet of women like Miranda – not those who exploit the trust placed in them, or technology companies that are crushingly slow to address the cruel misuse of their platforms, or legal systems that are still playing catch-up when it comes to issues such as image-based sexual abuse, otherwise known as 'revenge porn'.

Although claims of the empowering effects of social media abound, cases like Miranda's reveal their shaky foundations. In reality, social media can also be actively disempowering for women. On these platforms, judgement and shaming arise from multiple sources that centre around images and visibility, from a critical self-gaze to a misogynistic male gaze to the tracking and monitoring gaze of the technology that gobbles up user data and shadowy algorithms that dictate who gets to be seen and who doesn't, reproducing inequalities in the process. These gazes are funnelled through systems designed to normalise and encourage the surveillance of self and others, offering up a visual and emotional feast to get users hooked.

This presents a very real and difficult-to-solve conundrum. On the one hand, we live in a cultural moment where claiming visibility online is actively encouraged as a source of fun, as a means of conversation and engagement, as a way to be politically active, and, increasingly, as an economic imperative through which we 'market' ourselves in an ever more precarious climate. On the other hand, women claiming this visibility are often treated with suspicion. *Taking too many selfies, ladies? Expressing opinions no one asked you for? Desperate for attention, aren't you?* Or, as in Miranda's case, women are rendered responsible for the cultural meanings projected onto their image, even when it is used against them in ways they never intended, far beyond their original context. While the technology may be new, this victim-blaming impulse is not.

Writing about the conventions of the nude in classical European art, the critic John Berger observed how paintings were constructed to make their female subjects appear complicit, by inviting a desiring male gaze.[11] This notion of complicity, the idea that women are active participants in their objectification and are therefore culpable for the attention and punishment meted out to them, not only persists today – in some respects it has become heightened. It is the logic of those of ill-intent – 'bad actors' – who interpret a woman's choice to use these technologies as a provocation in which she is wilfully participating; a provocation that must be met with force if the status quo is to be upheld. In the twenty-first century the desire to simply be seen and heard can still render women guilty for eliciting the reactions of those who want nothing more than to shut them up and to demean them in the process. Like victim-blaming, these impulses are far from new. Back in the sixteenth century women were condemned to wear an iron muzzle known as a 'scold's bridle' for being judged rude or nagging or otherwise making a spectacle of themselves. Designed to both humiliate and torture, the bridle covered the head and flattened the tongue, taking away the offender's ability to speak and marking them as a figure for ridicule. In the twenty-first century, for women on the internet, the scold's bridle has gone digital.

On a yellow Post-It note over my desk where I worked on my doctoral thesis I'd written a quote from French philosopher Michel Foucault: 'Visibility is a trap.' The quote didn't make it into the final draft of the thesis but its sentiment, how the sense of being watched can be used to discipline people and get people to discipline themselves, seemed to me to capture tensions many users experience trying to navigate social media.

The quote comes from one of Foucault's famous works, *Discipline and Punish: The Birth of the Prison*. In it, he writes about a type of internalised surveillance he called 'panopticisim' designed to produce compliant, easily controlled subjects.[12] These subjects are governed not by external threats of punishment such as the guillotine or the stocks but by an internalised discipline produced through surveillance. To describe how it works, he referred to a model prison called the panopticon (a term that means 'seeing all'), which comprises a central tower around which the prisoners' cells circle. Foucault developed his ideas from the work of Victorian social reformer Jeremy Bentham, who saw the panoptic potential not just of prisons but other institutions including schools and hospitals; places that could be designed to produce more perfect societies through what he called 'a new mode of obtaining power of mind over mind'.[13] As Foucault outlines, the neat trick of the panopticon is that from the central tower it is possible for the prison guard to see directly into each cell at any given time without divulging their presence, leaving prisoners unsure as to if or when they are being observed. He writes, 'They are like so many cages, so many small theatres, in which each actor is alone, perfectly individualised and constantly visible.'[14] This results in a sense of perpetual, internalised surveillance on behalf of prisoners, meaning that even if the tower is empty, they act as if they are being watched just in case. In doing so, they adjust their behaviour to avoid what they sense to be an ever-present threat of punishment.

Today, as many scholars and cultural commentators have highlighted, smartphones and social media function as hand-held, mini panopticons, always with us, facilitating what is known as 'social surveillance'. This refers to the ways users watch each other online, producing an effect where they, as communications scholar Alice Marwick writes, 'strategically reveal, disclose and conceal personal information to create connections with others'[15]. We are now so accustomed to this interpersonal surveillance that we rarely stop to think about how the anticipation of being seen online actively shapes how we edit ourselves for digital audiences, whether they be real or imagined. We also don't dwell for too long on how much watching others online has come to stand in for real-world interaction, swapping phone calls and coffees for 'likes', retweets, generalised lurking and the endless scroll. Systematic surveillance is no longer the preserve of corporations and governments alone: it has become mainstreamed, normalised, something we do to ourselves and each other. Without realising it, we have been trained to use social media as a form of participatory watchfulness that allows us to 'see' what those who matter to us are doing, be they family or celebrities, and as a substitute for in-person interactions. In turn, we accept letting ourselves be seen, even when it feels uncomfortable. We watch ourselves and we watch each other through technology that is watching us all.

In the social media panopticon the role of the guard is performed in different ways. Firstly, by technology companies who trace and track users' every move, archiving (and profiting from) the content and data their online activities produce. These companies also design the platforms, setting the terms under which users are watched and watch others in turn. In this sense, users themselves act as guards within predefined parameters, monitoring their own behaviour and that of others. The platforms where all this watching takes place resemble what Foucault calls a 'file without end',[16] archiving – and therefore making visible and searchable to others – users' activities. Digital data is particularly suited for the archiving impulse Foucault describes because it is easily created and stored, reproduced, shared, copied and accessed. Users are free to leave social media (and the internet more broadly) whenever they want, but actually leaving – like leaving Hotel California – is difficult. As the saying goes, the internet never forgets.

Once an image is uploaded it can be impossible to ever remove it fully. This is what makes surveillance so different from merely looking. Whereas a look is ephemeral, existing only in the moment or in a memory, surveillance creates a record. These records form the bases of structures that gather information about people, typically with a view to understanding them and controlling them. Every online activity, from a quick internet search to a snarky tweet, creates a record, known as 'data', that tell technology companies more about us than perhaps our friends and family know. They also leave what Marwick calls 'digital traces',[17] which reveal us to those we know and those we don't. While much of this data is (for now) stored in out-of-reach servers, as the misappropriation of Lauren Miranda's selfie shows, it can resurface at any time, to be used in ways a user could never have expected.

For Foucault, visibility is a trap because it lends itself to disciplining people in ways that are subtle and therefore very effective for those in charge. This is because the individual internalises the surveillance to which they suspect, rightly or wrongly, they are being subjected, and this becomes a determining factor in how they behave. No brute force is required. Whether the guard is present or not is irrelevant: what matters is how the anticipation of being watched, under the real or imagined threat of punishment, motivates people to conform. This produces a contradiction with which users grapple every time they log on. The internet – and social media in particular – sells itself as a space where people are free to express themselves, unencumbered by the gatekeeping and speech restrictions of legacy media such as newspapers and television. But at the same time, every day online, users are reminded of how slippery and unpredictable the internet is. Unsurprisingly, this is a 'trap' into which most people want to avoid falling – but in doing so, they risk tripping into another.

In trying to avoid the tumult of public shaming and disagreement, most users try to anticipate judgement by presenting themselves as the right kind of person for whatever audience they anticipate will be viewing their content. But this drive to avoid punishment can be a breeding ground for conformity and paranoia, where people strive to balance their desire for visibility and authenticity with the possibility of judgement without ever fully escaping the threat of it. This is because users' quest for social approval is a significant part of what powers these platforms: but you can't have approval without judgement, and judgement can move in either direction.

For social approval to have worth, you must invest yourself in the external validation system that social media represents; you must believe that those hearts and follower counts represent real value. It's part of the reason many selfies are so similar and why we can refer to phenomena such as the 'Instagram look' as a shorthand for a type of uniformity or standard. There is no armed guard loudly demanding that users present themselves in prescriptive ways, yet online that is often exactly what people do because it seems the safest, most socially acceptable option. We want to be seen, but not in a way that is likely to cause us harm.

The irony, of course, is that social media sells itself as a way to express ourselves, to *be* ourselves and to connect with others through this shared openness. This conveniently sidesteps how these platforms are designed to shape self-expression in line with the status quo and their own economic interests, subtly nudging users into predictable, quantifiable standards that can be easily interpreted for marketers and advertisers. It also ignores the high emotional, psychological and reputational costs endured by those who experience the dark side of online visibility and for whom the dynamic of the 'trap' is not only a metaphor but a lived experience.

This is especially true for women who experience disproportionate levels of harassment on social media platforms for daring to embrace the visibility they offer, for which they are punished on the basis of their gender along with other intersections of their identity such as race and class. In summer 2020, during the coronavirus lockdown, rates of image-based sexual abuse (the victims of which are most often women) soared in Europe. Speaking to the news agency Reuters, Johanna Nelles, executive secretary of the Istanbul Convention, a European treaty to prevent violence against women, summed up the situation by saying, 'As the world moves online ... women and girls are exposed to higher risks.'[18] This trend tallies with growing research findings that indicate striking differences between genders when it comes to harassment online. A 2017 report from the Pew Centre in the US[19] showed that young women are at a much higher risk of sexualised forms of abuse online compared to young men. The young women they interviewed also reported being harassed online at a rate double that of their male peers. Over half the young women surveyed reported receiving 'explicit images they did not ask for' through social media, which begs serious questions about consent and the kinds of sexual norms new technologies enable.

But the harassment itself is only part of the story: its impact is another. The Pew Centre reports that of the women they surveyed who have experienced online harassment, 35 per cent find the experience either 'extremely or very upsetting' at rates double those of men. Meanwhile in 2018 an Amnesty International report on what it called #ToxicTwitter[20] found that 23 per cent of the women polled from eight countries had experienced some form of harassment on the platform. This included threats of sexual and physical violence; identity-based abuse such as racism, transphobia or homophobia; sustained, targeted harassment and invasions of privacy. Outlining the fears and frustrations of the women they spoke to, Amnesty said, 'Women have the right to live free from discrimination and violence. They also have the right to freely express themselves, both online and offline. Twitter's policies and practices clearly fail to respect these rights.' As we will see throughout this book, Twitter's shortcomings are far from unique.

To better understand the particular ways women are vulnerable to the excesses of the visibility trap, we first need to explore the politics of visibility, especially as they relate to the quest for equality and women's place in public life. This is what cultural theorist bell hooks (who does not capitalise her name) refers to in the quote at the beginning of the chapter: there is indeed immense power in looking, but this power has not been enjoyed or exercised equally. The denial of women's visibility both in terms of their presence in the public sphere and the articulation of their perspectives is a critical aspect of inequality in whatever context it arises. Thus, it is important to emphasise that while digital technologies such as social media may be new, the ways in which gendered effects of the visibility trap seek to keep women in their place – while profiting off their visibility and labour – have roots that are millennia deep.

Images of women, meanwhile – particularly those of the light-skinned, youthful and conventionally attractive – have always had huge commercial power. They have also been used as cultural exemplars for what women should aspire to be, excluding the vast majority of women who neither look – nor particularly want to look – like a Californian beach goddess. This dissonance and its impact on self-esteem have long been used by advertisers and marketers to urge women to invest in their products. Today we live in a world that has never been more visual, one where images of women are no longer made almost exclusively by men. With digital technology, women can easily create and broadcast their own images and consume images of other women, but thanks to the machinations of the visibility trap, the radical potential of this development is often met with a desire to control representation rather than let it run free.

Throughout history, whenever and wherever women have entered the public sphere they have met with fulsome pushback. If we consider digital technology, and social media in particular, as a new form of public sphere or space, we see can how the surveillance and shaming used to control women in the past is being repackaged and reinvigorated today. To explore how present and past collide in these spaces, we're going to begin with bicycles and the Victorian ladies who first dared to cycle them; women who faced warnings about 'bicycle face' just as women today face warnings about 'tech face'. Then we'll turn to the immense commercial and aesthetic power of images of women and their fraught relationship to the flesh-and-blood women they are supposed to represent, a tension social media is celebrated as readdressing. The reality, as we will see, is much more complex.

In 1897 Cambridge University's then predominately male student body organised in their thousands to defend what they regarded as a serious threat to the integrity of the British educational system. The source of this threat? A controversial proposal put to the university's governors, arguing that woman students be awarded full degrees. So unthinkable was this development that on the day it was to be debated, a huge crowd gathered in Cambridge's Market Square to voice their displeasure.[21] They threw flour and eggs, holding banners aloft that read 'Varsity for Men'. Most spectacularly, they hung an effigy of a woman cyclist out a window near where the debate was taking place. When news of the proposal's defeat reached the protesters, historian Sheila Hanlon writes, 'the triumphant mob tore down the effigy. They then savagely attacked the mannequin, decapitating it and tearing it to pieces in a wild frenzy. The shredded remains of the poor lady cyclist were later stuffed through the gates of

Newnham College.'[22] At the time Newnham was one of only two female colleges in Cambridge so it's fair to assume this stunt was, at best, an expression of extreme displeasure, if not an outright threat.

Whenever I read that another woman has been hounded off the internet by baying sexists, I'm reminded of the misogynistic treatment doled out to the Cambridge effigy. The students' choice of mannequin and its enthusiastic destruction were no coincidence. Cycling had become not just about transport for women; it also symbolised their growing demands for equality and a life beyond the home. This included access to the public sphere and its worlds of education, government, employment and the arts. Today, in countries where female cyclists are common, it is a struggle to imagine the stir women on bikes caused when they first appeared in the late nineteenth century. If we think of technology as a tool that enables humans to master their environment, then the bicycle provided women with exciting and novel ways not only to travel but to exercise their independence. Pedalling women invaded streets, parks and the countryside, public spaces hitherto reserved for men, vexing those like the irate boys of Cambridge. Their presence signalled changing times and changing fashions, challenging long-established 'proper' order that regarded women, particularly those of the upper and middles classes, as fragile creatures best ensconced within the domestic sphere (to note, working-class women had long worked outside the home to provide for their families). Their boldness was met with visceral condemnation, including threats of physical violence. In 1897, the same year as the Cambridge protest, a female cyclist named Kitty described needing 'nerves of iron' to deal with verbal abuse when cycling in London. 'One needs to be very brave to stand all that,' she says in a letter, her exasperation clear. 'It makes one feel mad and ones [sic] ideas of humanity at large sink to a very low standard.'[23]

Given its conservatism and belief in rigid gender roles, Victorian society sought to curtail women's love of cycling. All sorts of reasons were put forward to keep women off their bikes. Perhaps the best one of all was a manufactured affliction known as 'bicycle face'[24] (I consider it as an early form of 'resting bitch face'[25] of which I am a long-time sufferer). Doctors postulated that, as a result of the physical rigours of cycling, women's faces grew tense and worn with gibbous eyes and gritted jaws. In other words, cycling made women deeply unattractive to heterosexual men and so they had better abandon it, *tout de suite*. We can laugh at the 'mad' Victorians, but consider this: in August 2016 the 'female' section of popular British news website the *Mail Online* published a piece entitled 'Do YOU have tech face? The weird ways your mobile phone is rapidly ageing your skin (and the clever ways you can fix it).'[26] Illustrated entirely by women staring at their phones, the piece warns female readers that smartphones are 'wreaking havoc with our faces', causing vague but ugly-sounding 'ailments' such as 'sagging jaws', 'squint lines' and something called 'tech neck'. Apparently, tech face, as with its precursor bicycle face, is highly gender specific as the piece *never mentions men*.

Just like social media, the bicycle brought women new freedoms that challenged the established order[27] (let's not forget that prior to digital cameras and smartphones, most images of women in popular culture were taken by men and the possibility for ordinary people to easily broadcast their daily life or political opinions was scarcely imaginable).

But alongside the benefits, these new freedoms also opened up women to fresh gender-based surveillance and judgement. In a similar way, while social media can certainly be used to advance women's status, it also enables forces that seek to commodify and control this freedom for their own ends. It is why tech companies are so quick to offer women 'empowerment' through products of questionable intent, like beauty apps, but are so desperately slow to address sexist and racial abuse on their platforms. Why this is the case comes down to the complex relationship between visibility, equality and power at a moment when, as never before, previously marginalised people all over the world are representing themselves in this new public space we call 'social media', many of whom are creating vast amounts of an item that has always made folks hot, bothered, intensely voyeuristic and in some cases, very rich: images of women.

In 1914 suffragette Mary Richardson walked into the National Gallery in London, armed with a knife. An eyewitness reported that Richardson stood in front of the *Rokeby Venus*, aka *Venus With the Mirror*, 'for some moments, apparently in contemplation of it' before slashing the canvas. In an account published in the *Times* the next day, Richardson stated, 'I have tried to destroy the picture of the most beautiful woman in mythological history as a protest against the Government for destroying Mrs. Pankhurst, who is the most beautiful character in modern history.'[28] She added, 'Justice is an element of beauty as much as colour and outline on canvas.'[29]

Richardson's protest was firstly about drawing attention to the unfair incarceration of Emmeline Pankhurst, a hero of the suffragette movement. It also highlighted the hypocrisy of a patriarchal society that was happy to feast on images of women in various stages of undress but declined, often violently, to allow actual women their rights. Richardson's choice of the *Rokeby Venus* shows how valuable images of women as a commodity were and continue to be. The painting, considered a masterpiece, depicts the goddess Venus as pale, youthful and nude, reclining with her back to the spectator, staring at her reflection in a mirror held aloft by a cherub. In 1911 the painting was valued at £45,000, the equivalent of £4,860,000 in today's money.[30]

You don't need a degree in art history or economics to know that idealised images of women like the *Rokeby* remain hugely valuable, both in cultural and economic terms, to such a degree that the sociologist Gaye Tuchman once called them 'the primary commodity object of Western visual culture'.[31] Social media offers business even more new ways to exploit our fascination with the female image, with concerning outcomes for women. Just ask L'Oréal CEO Jean-Paul Agon. According to a report in the UK's *Daily Telegraph*, Agon is thrilled with the way Instagram prompts women to buy more make-up to try and match how they look in real life with edited images of themselves online. 'If they want to use filters to look better online, they have to do something in real life also to look better,' he reportedly said, 'and that is why they use more cosmetics, more make-up, more skin care, more everything.'[32] Where some of us see a worrying intensification of beauty pressure and conformity in our hyper-visual age, Monsieur Agon sees only euro signs.

Consider how much revenue images of women and women's labour generates for companies such as Facebook, for whom Instagram, which it bought in 2012, is now worth a staggering $100 billion.[33] After all, women are the biggest users of both platforms, and Mark Zuckerberg understands only too well the captivating effects of mixing visual and digital culture. Who can forget his early foray into website development as a student with the infamous 'Facemash'?

Using a judgemental gaze now so familiar from social media, the site invited Harvard students to rate their peers 'hot or not', using profile pictures Zuckerberg hacked from a university web server (note the disregard for consent). Facemash was ultimately shut down only after outcry from, among others, the Association of Harvard Black Women.[34] When testifying before members of the US Congress in 2018 in the aftermath of the Cambridge Analytica scandal, Zuckerberg was asked about Facemash. 'You put up pictures of two women and decided which one was more attractive of the two, is that right?' asked Representative Billy Long. 'Congressman, that is an accurate description of the prank website I made when I was a sophomore,' Zuckerberg replied.[35]

Sites like Facemash and Instagram, as with so much social media, feed into our fascination with the visual. Humans *love* to look but the way in which we look and how we are looked at depends very much on where we are situated in a cultural and political sense. On holiday one year I visited Munich's stunning Nymphenburg Palace, summer home of the Wittelsbach dynasty, former rulers of Bavaria. I wandered into what is somewhat creepily known as the Gallery of Beauties[36], featuring thirty-six portraits of attractive young women painted between 1827 and 1850 at the request of the highly sexed King Ludwig I of Bavaria, who collected the paintings for his personal enjoyment. Many of the women featured had at one time been conquests of Ludwig's. Among them was the notorious Irish courtesan Lola Montez, Italian philosophy scholar the Marchesa Marianna Florenzi and Josepha Conti, Bavarian servant and renowned beauty, whose eyes-to-heaven expression made me speculate as to how much she enjoyed having her portrait painted.

A rich and influential man, Ludwig is representative of those who, throughout history, could commission and buy paintings at will. In other words, Ludwig's ability to look was predicated on his power as a wealthy male and as a monarch. The women he had painted did not share this power. As John Berger notes,[37] the patronage system in European art was predominately male-dominated, whereby a wealthy man would pay the artist – also usually a man – to paint for him. Given that the artist was relying on his patron to fund his work, he found ways to flatter him. Often this involved painting females who were aesthetically pleasing and untroubling to his male gaze, he being the subject, she being the object, a motif that is replicated in all kinds of visual culture up to the present day. This led Berger to make his most famous observation: 'men *act* and women *appear*. Men look at women. Women watch themselves being looked at. This determines not only most relations between men and women but also the relation of women to themselves.'[38] Although this dynamic has not gone away, by democratising the tools of self-representation social media has challenged the subject–object opposition. The images of women we see each day are now more likely to have been made by women themselves. Not only that, rather than being passive or voiceless, these images often come with the opinions and personalities of their creators attached. Rather than being defined by the male gaze, they meet it and talk back.

Earlier I mentioned Berger's points on complicity and how classical paintings were composed to make women appear complicit in the attention foisted upon them. Here's how he describes it: 'You painted a naked woman because you enjoyed looking at her, put a mirror in her hand and you called the painting "Vanity," thus morally condemning the woman whose nakedness you had depicted for you own pleasure.'[39] I think of this quote whenever I am confronted by the *Mail Online*'s notorious 'sidebar of shame', a key element of its homepage, helping to make it one of the most visited news sites in the world. The sidebar primarily functions as a vicious celebrity gossip blog where commenters feast on image-heavy stories, predominantly about women. Originally filled with paparazzi shots, the sidebar now also includes images drawn from the social media accounts of women who may or may not have previously been in the public eye and who may or may not object to their image being used in this way. This type of content is inexpensive and accessible: and in an age of declining advertising revenue and an insatiable 24/7 news cycle (the internet never closes), that matters. Selling notions of female complicity to the ogling masses is as cheap as chips and for some, just as appetising. In sidebar parlance, a woman does not simply wear clothes or walk down the street or post a selfie. She 'flaunts', she 'exposes', she 'pours', she 'reveals', she 'shows off'. God help her if she wants to look nice in a dress every so often or has the audacity to age or takes her chances trying to profit off the male gaze's fascination with her. By becoming visible through endeavour or achievement, online spaces like the sidebar send a depressingly familiar message to celebrity women and every woman watching: put up or shut up, because we know you love it really.

From the Victorian pedal-pushers to women with opinions on the internet today, claiming visibility for women remains a complicated affair. On the one hand, achieving visibility can be a gamechanger for representation, for equality, for progress. On the other hand, visibility invites ever more sophisticated forms of scrutiny and discipline, while images of women, endlessly proliferating and circulating in the name of profit, are a constant reminder of all the ways actual women fail to measure up to what society prescribes as the 'ideal'. Social theorist Patricia Hill Collins notes the controlling nature of these kinds of popular images, and how they hold immense cultural and political power when it comes to shaping representations of women along gender, racial and class lines.[40] This produces a tension that is not easily resolved; one we need to be aware of now more than ever because into this mix sashays social media, draped in the glittering promises of progress, allowing us to see and be seen like no technology before.

We are told that thanks to Snapchat, TikTok, Instagram and Facebook we have more control over our image, particularly when it comes to how others see us – assertions that are, as we will see, questionable to say the least. In our image-obsessed culture, claiming visibility online is presented as an inherently good thing with which users should hop on board, a move that conveniently sidesteps the parts of social media visibility – the trap, as I call it – that are not 'good things'. For starters, for those without other forms of cultural capital to draw on, chasing emotional fulfilment or financial success through these new tools of self-representation can be a daunting, time-consuming task that yields little in the way of reward. It requires that users submit themselves to 'always-on' levels of visibility and that they give them their attention ceaselessly, from the moment they grope for their phones in the morning to when they set their alarms at night. Social media has no 'off' switch. The emphasis it places on status means chasing likes is non-negotiable. These activities have been so thoroughly sold to us as recreational and convenient that we don't stop to consider them as a form of work. Perhaps we should.

Every day, as users, we watch and are watched, our behaviour tracked and influenced in subtle but invasive ways by technologies that offer themselves as neutral, even friendly. But the technology is not the only thing tracking us: other people are too, in ways that are fond and charitable and also in ways that are anything but. Social media presents this new normal as progress, where the messy aspects of rising levels of judgement and surveillance in our lives are glossed over by jokey terms – think 'FOMO' and 'TMI' – treating legitimate emotional responses with a disconcerting, superficial lightness. Users are expected to know, as if by instinct, how much of themselves they should reveal and how best to perform their lives to secure the wildly disparate approval of friends, family, employers, lovers and strangers, while still managing – somehow! – to appear 'authentic'. When the mask of digital perfection slips, as it inevitably will, individual 'sin' is turned into a spectacle, whether of the explosive pile-on variety or of the quieter though no less acerbic picking-apart of screenshots in private messages and Facebook groups. Social media has turned interpersonal surveillance into something we do for fun, a form of sport that can be hard to critique since all users are guilty by association.

This intense focus Western culture places on visibility in the digital age is often sold to women in particular as an 'empowering' opportunity, rather than an additional burden. 'You can't be what you can't see,' is a common refrain that captures the power of representation, drawing attention to the many who, by virtue of their race, gender, class, sexuality or ability, have traditionally been excluded from visibility in the media, in politics and in our institutions. But what if the visibility promised to women by social media trades on this injustice without delivering the transformation that it demands? What if, in offering new tools for self-representation, these technologies are also reinvigorating the very forces that sought to exclude women from public life by not only rejecting the demand for equality but also by attacking those who make it? And what if, in encouraging users to examine their appearance in ever more forensic ways and to endlessly compare themselves to others, these technologies are contributing to sharply rising levels of depression, anxiety and poor body image in young women?[41]

When used to fight for political causes that impact women's lives and health, social media visibility can be galvanising. I could, for example, write a list as long as my leg of hashtags from different parts of the world drawing urgent attention to grassroots campaigns fighting for equality. Among those that have provoked coverage, debate and solidarity, online and offline, are #MeToo (international, inspired by the foundational work of civil rights activist Tarana Burke), #EverydaySexism (started by Laura Bates in the UK and now international), #SayHerName (drawing attention to police brutality to black women in the US), #GirlsLikeUs (US, supporting trans visibility online), #KoreaToo (South Korea's response to the #MeToo movement), #BalanceTonPorc (France, translating as 'get rid of your pig'), #NiUnaMenos (South American campaign to end gender-based violence, translating from Spanish as 'not one [woman] less'), #MyCameraisMyWeapon and #WhiteWednesday (campaigning against sexual harassment and Iran's mandatory hijab law), #effyourbeautystandards (a rallying cry of the body positivity movement), #NowforNI (Northern Ireland, fighting for abortion rights), #Repealthe8th (Republic of Ireland, part of a successful grassroots campaign that overhauled Ireland's draconian abortion regime) and Poland's Czarny Poniedziałek (translated as 'Black Monday', campaigning for abortion rights in the face of an increasingly powerful conservative government).

Women who felt out of step with the world and those who have been denied visibility in other aspects of their lives have found much-needed community and kinship online; the kind I could only dream about growing up in rural Ireland, as the only feminist in the village. But all this online visibility has not halted serious rollbacks on women's rights in recent years, whether it is the mounting threat to legal abortion in the US or the decimation of domestic violence and rape-crisis services under Ireland and the UK's austerity policies or the environmental degradation fought on the front lines by indigenous women across the world. Online visibility can also produce an over-focus on the self and individualised notions of 'feeling good' that can be counterproductive to activist aims.

In early 2021 I spoke with the writer and activist Aubrey Gordon of Your Fat Friend[42] fame about changes in discourse around body positivity since the rise of social media, a trend the pandemic has intensified. 'So there's this explosion of interest but it's an explosion of interest in what social media users want to believe the movement is without actual regard to the movement's history and who has led it and what its goals have been,' she said, referring to the origins of the body positivity and fat-acceptance movements in the counterculture of the sixties and seventies.

Pointing out that body positivity 'is a movement that predates social media and ideally will outlive it', Gordon explained:

> The focus gets really, really lost because folks see hashtags or short phrases or tweets or whatever and bring their own aspirational thinking to it and project their own expectations onto whatever they expect it to be, which makes it really, really hard to trace the history of a movement [and] to maintain some level of focus on shared goals.
>
> It means you're constantly in this place of going back to square one [...]: no, no, no, no – here's what it is. Here's where it comes from. No, no, no, no. That's not what it is. It's not like, you feel bad and you should feel good. It's that there are concrete, systemic barriers to some kinds of bodies that other kinds of bodies don't face.

Greater degrees of visibility for women of the kind offered by social media do not automatically translate into more equality or material change: in fact, this visibility may even create more problems than it solves. When a young Saudi woman, Rahaf Mohammed al-Qunun, fled the country in early 2019 to escape its notorious male guardianship laws, she opened a Twitter account to appeal to the international community for asylum. Tens of thousands of followers later, the world paid attention; Rahaf now lives safely in Canada.[43] In the aftermath of her escape, a Saudi official was recorded jokingly asking why authorities had not confiscated Rahaf's phone instead of her passport 'because Twitter changed everything', he'd chuckled, ominously.[44]

Rahaf's story shows the undeniable potential social media has to command and mobilise vast amounts of attention and energy on a global level. But its downsides are undeniable too. While social media certainly provides a platform, it can't guarantee every user-in-need the level of visibility required to create change. Thankfully, Rahaf's tweets were not swallowed up by the rolling maul of online content, but how many cries for help are? And why, in the twenty-first century, should women have to resort to shouting into the digital abyss to get their needs met and their rights upheld?

At the heart of the visibility trap is how social media extends old forms of gender-based surveillance and enables new ones, creating new ways of seeing that are not always as progressive as they first appear. For women, this can be particularly unforgiving. As media studies professor Lisa Nakamura writes, 'There is no form of surveillance that is innocent.'[45] This is especially true for minorities for whom surveillance at the hands of the state and other institutions has meant objectification, discrimination and restrictions on freedom.

Around the time of Rahaf's escape, despite outcry from human-rights organisations, Apple was 'reviewing' while Google was continuing to support (via its store) an app that enables Saudi men grant or deny the women in their charge the right to travel.[46] The app works by tracking an individual's movements through their phone. For a young woman in the position Rahaf found herself in, this is surely a terrifying and potentially deathly-dangerous development, one which illustrates the troubling dark side of digital technology and the vulnerability that is part and parcel of increased visibility. According to *The New York Times*, the name of the app, Absher, loosely translates as 'yes, sir'.[47] At the time of writing in 2021, Absher is still available to download on both Apple's and Google's app stores.

Early in March 2020, after four long years, I finally finished my doctoral study. Just a week later the pandemic hit. Overnight, as people scrambled to make sense of our new reality, digital technologies became an even greater force in modern life. In the midst of this sea change I quickly realised that the trends I had spent so long thinking about were set to intensify. Around the same time, in an open letter to mark the thirty-first anniversary of the World Wide Web (or 'the internet' as we know it today) its inventor, the British engineer Tim Berners-Lee, issued a stark warning: 'the web is not working for women and girls'.[48] Calling for an internet that is 'safe, empowering and available to all', Berners-Lee said that he was 'seriously concerned' about 'online harms facing women and girls – especially those of colour, from LGBTQ+ communities and other marginalised groups'.[49] For him, the scale of these harms is an active threat to the gains of equality. This includes the internet access gap between men and women, the level of online harassment faced by girls and women and the role of artificial intelligence such as algorithms in perpetuating sexist, racist and other harmful stereotypes.

It is difficult to imagine but the internet we have today could have looked very different. In the early days of the World Wide Web, tech utopians, among them early cyberfeminists,[50] dreamt of a space where our offline selves melted away, enabling human consciousness to roam virtual worlds, guided by curiosity and playfulness, free from the baggage of history and discrimination. Fanciful though these ideas may have been, they showed a bold ambition for what the internet could be. This ambition was rooted in the hope that through technology, humanity could find new ways of relating to one another, unencumbered by inequality or the limits of identity. But as the Web became more commercialised, this freewheeling vision was gradually replaced. Today, given its obsession with metrics, status and enormous profits, instead of transcending identity, social media amplifies it, creating online environments characterised by intense watchfulness, competitiveness, distrust and disagreement, where images rule all. Meanwhile, data collection, which is so central to social media's profit model, means users are endlessly profiled and categorised. This information is then boxed up and delivered to advertisers through the kinds of invasive surveillance processes early net utopians could only have imagined in their darkest nightmares.

Digital technologies promise a lot and in some ways they deliver. When we cannot be physically present with those we love, when we need information quickly, when we want to relax with videos of cute cats doing stupid things, the internet provides. But in doing so, technologies like social media require that users expose the most intimate aspects of themselves, their desires, disappointments, vulnerabilities, memories and relationships. This is a very different way to consume media than how we did it in the twentieth century. Back then, ye olde media like television or the radio broadcast *at* consumers – occasionally counting them to figure out which of their offerings were most popular. With the internet we are simultaneously being broadcasted to while *broadcasting ourselves* – communication is now suddenly going both ways, all day long, creating a vast archive and network of human interaction that can be used for good or, just as easily, for bad. We watch and are watched, learning to observe ourselves and others in ever more forensic ways as 'seeing' each other through technology becomes normal rather than novel. Online, we are all voyeurs for whom the twitching curtain or the peephole is now our screens, an appealing space of 'likes', 'community' and 'followers' but one where the spectre of judgement and disgrace is constant. The trap is only ever a click away.

Two

Self/ie

In November 2015 Australian social influencer Essena O'Neill committed what appeared to be spectacular career suicide. The then eighteen-year-old posted a video that quickly went viral, sparking headlines across the internet. In it, a tearful O'Neill revealed she had decided to quit social media.[1] This announcement might not have garnered the attention it did were it not for the fact that O'Neill occupied the upper echelons of online celebrity, enjoying what appeared to be a lucrative career with hundreds of thousands of followers across platforms such as Instagram and YouTube. It also helped that O'Neill embodied aesthetics with which the Western media (social media included) is routinely enamoured: youthful, white, conventionally attractive and vulnerable. 'What I'm doing scares the absolute fuck out of me. I don't know where I'm going, I don't know what's going to happen next,' she says in the video. The raw emotion in her voice reflects the stripped-back simplicity of her surroundings, her tear-stained, make-up-free face contrasting sharply with the usually sunny hues of influencer culture. She adds that she hopes her decision will be 'a wake-up call' to those who follow her.

In cultural terms O'Neill's video can be read as a classic cautionary tale updated for our digital age; a warning about those who fall prey to the allure of dubious riches. (As Chapter Four will discuss, dramatically exiting the internet has become, over the last five years or so, something of a trope for influencers, but I prefer to think of it as rejecting visibility or negotiating with it, something many users do in different ways and for different reasons.) There is no question that O'Neill's online career won her glittering material success (the path to which social media is credited in some quarters as democratising). This included modelling contracts in her native Australia and the US, sponsorship deals for clothing and cosmetics, and invitations to travel the globe. Yet for O'Neill, social media success also brought loneliness, crushingly low self-esteem and a profound sense of disconnection from the world. 'I'm the girl who had it all,' she acknowledges in her farewell video, her voice breaking, 'and I'm here to tell you that having it all on social media means absolutely nothing.'

In a pandemic-hit world where many of us are relying on social media as never before while also questioning its outsized place in our lives, O'Neill's video feels like a foretelling. Throughout, she draws distinctions between her offline and online life, highlighting the gap between the two as a major source of her distress. O'Neill talks about the pressure of 'living in a screen', of wanting to be 'a perfect person online', where 'everything I did was for views, for likes, for followers'. This results in feeling detached from herself and those around her, the demands of social media bleeding into her free time, including her relationships with friends and family. 'I don't know who I am,' she says. 'I don't know what I stand for.'

The gap O'Neill identifies between her off- and online selves captures a key aspect of the visibility trap: how the intense use of these technologies and learning to see ourselves through them can fragment our sense of self. Most of us now carry small but terribly powerful computers. These technologies bring many benefits but they also, by design, encourage users to compare themselves to others and, increasingly, to their computer-generated selves, on a scale unimaginable just a decade ago. Getting the likes that represent social approval often means engaging in strategic acts of self-expression that may or may not be a fair and accurate representation of who we are. Often, it can feel like we are moving ever closer to a world such as the one portrayed in the 'Nosedive' episode of the *Black Mirror* series,[2] where access to everything from housing to healthcare is predicated on one's social media ranking, leading people to behave in bizarre and self-interested ways that are ultimately unsustainable. When we fail to measure up to our computer-generated 'best selves' or win the desired level of approval – human beings are, after all, made of flesh not filters – not only do we know it and see it, but other people do, too. This takes the shame of impostor syndrome to a deeply discomforting new level. The grubbiness of feeling like a fraud spreads beyond a bad day at work, stirring whenever we log in and even when we don't.

For all its positives, the unpleasant truth about participatory technologies is that they encourage us to judge often and to judge hard. But in doing so, we also learn to judge ourselves in ever more finite ways. Apps and filters allow us to perfect our selfies but they also draw our attention, again and again, to the distance between how we are and how we long to be. Flaws we never knew existed are now captured and magnified by sophisticated cameras which, just a decade ago, would have been considered something from a sci-fi novel. The more we invest ourselves in this system, the more we become haunted by the posed, digitally altered images of ourselves we have created in which we look as we desire to be but know, to our shame, we are not. Even though we understand that what we see online is highly stylised and performative, routinely comparing ourselves to others and to our own 'perfect' pictures can take a heavy emotional toll. The results can be detrimental for a user's self-esteem, body image and well-being.

O'Neill's video was not her only attempt to showcase how unhappy social media made her and the fragmented reality into which it plunged her. On her Instagram she recaptioned selfies and other shots to reveal the huge amount of work and time that had gone into creating an image that looked effortlessly beautiful. In one such selfie, O'Neill smiles into the camera. She is made-up and fashionably dressed, appearing to welcome the gaze of her audience. But the recaption on the image tells a very different story:

> Please like this photo. I put make-up on, curled my hair, tight dress, big uncomfortable jewellery ... Took over 50 shots until I got one I think you might like, then I edited this one selfie for ages on several apps – just so I could feel some social approval from you. THERE IS NOTHING REAL ABOUT THIS. #celebrityconstruct[3]

The caption on this selfie is striking for a number of reasons. First, for the sharp contrast O'Neill's honesty makes clear – despite appearances, there is nothing about this image that is remotely effortless. Second, for the way it directly addresses whoever may be watching, illustrating the intensely visual nature of the exchange on Instagram between creator and spectator. O'Neill outlines the ways in which the anticipation of an audience motivates her actions, influencing how she represents herself and, as a consequence, how she *sees* herself. It is an anticipation many a user of social media will understand all too well. Far from being authentic, this is an image designed for other people. It might be called a 'selfie' but, in many ways, the self takes a backseat. Instead, the subject undertakes masses of work to figure out and conform to what she senses is expected of her. Even then, there is no guarantee that she will achieve the social approval she craves. She may even be criticised, and harshly. So she works harder, taking more and more pictures to appease a nebulous, judgemental shadow-figure who she knows and yet does not know. 'I let myself be defined by numbers,' O'Neill says in her video, adding with a sigh, 'it was never enough.'

From the earliest studies of the phenomenon, women have shown a marked predilection for selfie-taking.[4] While this trend is often scoffed at as cultural practices coded 'feminine' often are, for those who have traditionally been denied the ability to represent themselves or who see themselves endlessly misrepresented, technologies like the selfie are an important tool for talking back and taking up space. But this claiming of visibility also raises questions of power. As stories like Lauren Miranda's and O'Neill's show, cultural attitudes to selfies hold up a digital mirror to contemporary tensions around gender and representation. As such, they are a prime locale for observing the visibility trap in action, where the best of social media intersects with some of the worst.

A large part of my doctoral study explored everyday experiences of the selfie phenomenon. A key motivation for this was trying to gain a more nuanced understanding of the selfie's appeal to young women against the predictable and largely untested claims made in popular discourse. One of these claims, oft repeated, is that women's proclivity for selfie use is down to plain old narcissism. There are a number of issues with this, the first being that when these assumptions began to circulate circa 2013, the phenomenon was so new it was impossible to say with any veracity (from an academic perspective) if this were true. Research can take years and even then, findings can be inconclusive or contradictory. But that didn't stop talking heads from drawing expectable but untested conclusions about the phenomenon, the kind that relied heavily on Berger's idea of female complicity. Over time, these conclusions have solidified into a kind of 'common sense' that can obscure the complexities at play while overlooking the fact that there is so much we have yet to understand about the impact of new technologies on our lives.

For now, let's take a critical look at narcissism as an explanation for women's love of the selfie, it being a term that is taken to characterise our age as perhaps no other. Of course, at its most excessive, narcissism is not just a descriptor – it is a disorder, ironically, a rather ugly one. If you've ever had the misfortune to knowingly encounter someone with an actual narcissistic personality disorder, you'll understand how trying the afflicted can be. You might also be aware of how difficult such conditions are to diagnose in a clinical sense and that they represent the extreme, not the norm. All of which is to say, narcissism, as a concept, is often bandied about in our current climate without the necessary gradation to make discussions about it meaningful and, by extension, impactful. Women's use of the selfie is a classic example. All too regularly, the narcissism label gets slapped on without stopping to consider, firstly, why femininity is so automatically aligned with narcissism in the first place, and secondly, the complicated and often negative relationship many women have to their image, which is as far from narcissistic as one can possibly get.

In the original Greek myth Narcissus was a young man, renowned for his beauty, who fell in love with his own reflection. Thanks to the machinations of male dominance, over time narcissism and vanity have become associated with femininity rather than masculinity, with consequences for real women as much as symbolic ones. This arrangement is far from new. The art historian Frances Borzello outlines how the tribulations faced by early women artists battling their way into the male-dominated art world stemmed from societies that viewed female ambition as unbecoming, even deviant.[5] This essentially meant that women artists had to do two jobs: firstly, the not insignificant work of the artist, and secondly, gender work, meaning they endeavoured to present themselves and their paintings in ways that would not draw the ire of those predisposed to judge them for being a woman. To critics, it was unnatural that a woman should want to be an artist, putting her work and therefore *herself* ahead of her 'proper' role as a wife and mother. By extension, female artists' supposed proclivity for the self-portrait was read as 'evidence' of inherent narcissism and self-obsession. As Borzello writes:

> The ideal of the female affinity for self-portraiture may have drawn strength from the personification

> of the vice of vanity, and is in fact a subtle insult. Since vanity was for centuries personified as a woman looking in a mirror, a female self-portrait is evidence of this female vice …[6]

The millions of selfies taken by women each day may not be art, but, as Borzello's remarks show, their reception tells us a great deal about long-time attitudes to women's attempts to make themselves seen, whether through art or politics or simply by refusing to be treated like a doormat. Part of this quest for visibility has always required that women 'do' femininity in the right way so as not to upset the delicate sensibilities of the gender police. As far back as 1929 the psychoanalyst Joan Riviere developed the theory of 'the feminine masquerade' to outline how women use femininity as a mask that allows them entry into the public sphere.[7] By appearing to play by the rules while trying to flout them, women attempt to wrangle power for themselves, outwardly conforming to the feminine performance expected of them. While this approach may bear some fruit, ultimately it keeps women shackled to notions of femininity that can limit and underserve them; the kind that prompt hisses of 'who does she think she is?' whenever a woman steps outside her prescribed role. Ninety years after Riviere's essay, female politicians still have to juggle their official duties with the disproportionate attention paid to their appearance. It is a pretty dismal indictment of how far we still have to go that saying, 'Sod it, if Boris Johnson can't be bothered to brush his hair, why should I?' is not an option for any female politician who wants to be taken seriously.

Writing in *The Second Sex*, one of the grand tomes of Western feminism, the philosopher Simone de Beauvoir devotes an entire chapter to the issue of – you've guessed it – narcissism.[8] De Beauvoir argues that narcissism is regarded by society as 'the fundamental attitude of all women'. But then she does something that we should all endeavour to do. Rather than simply accepting what society tells her is the case, she asks *why* society is trying to sell her this idea in the first place. She comes up with an interesting theory for why women are more likely to display what seem to be narcissistic behaviours compared to men, which has less to do with any essentialist notion of what a woman is and more to do with what society expects her to be. 'Woman,' de Beauvoir writes, 'as a subject, is frustrated by her lack of freedom ... she is not recognised as an individual in her own right.'[9] With few other options open to her, the woman turns her attentions inward rather than outward, her fantasies and desires becoming orientated around the self rather than the wider world, her access to which is limited. In a passage that is as beautiful as it is moving in its articulation of a female desire for autonomy and control over one's life, de Beauvoir writes: 'Every woman drowned in her reflection reigns over space and time, alone, sovereign; she has total rights over men, fortune, glory, and sensual pleasure.'[10] Things have progressed a great deal for women in the West since the forties when de Beauvoir was writing, but there is something about this insight that still resonates. Just like the mirror before it, today our screens represent a similar type of psychological escape, where, however fleetingly, we can become our idealised, supreme selves, at least in our own minds.

Picking at the issue of narcissism, then, reveals it to be an extremely knotty affair. While rates of narcissism are rising in Western societies, the reasons for this are complex, with roots that go much further back than the arrival of social media.[11,12] The changing economic landscape of the nineteenth century, for example, saw major demographic fluctuations as large numbers of people swapped rural, agricultural living for life in urban areas. With this shift (along with the rise of advertising and the mass media) the individual, rather than the family, class or community they were born into, became the primary way through which people were encouraged to experience the world. This increased emphasis on the self and individuality characterised much of twentieth-century popular culture in the West. Reinforced by consumerism, it urged people to think of themselves, first and foremost, in terms of their image and status, using the kind of logic once reserved for commodities. Social media has intensified this trend tenfold, where marketing terminology is applied not to products but to the self. Living *your* best life. Achieving *your* dreams. Developing *your* personal brand.

Social media not only follows these long-standing trends; it disseminates and normalises them like no media before. It takes the norms of celebrity, once reserved for only the most visible people in our culture, and makes them everyday. Image-management is now something everyone with a social media account is expected to perform, where the fifteen minutes of fame Andy Warhol prophesised is achieved via likes, retweets, comments and shares.[13] On platforms designed to orientate entirely around reputation and the self, visibility requires that users endlessly give of themselves in the form of attention, opinions, images, emotion and so on. Online it's all about 'me, me, me!' – not necessarily because humanity is going to hell in a handbasket but because the individualised pursuit of status is what social media is designed to encourage and reward.[14] This is no accident. The more we reveal about ourselves, the juicier and more valuable our data becomes and the more content there is for other users to feast on and vice versa – all of which is fantastic news for social media companies' primary concern: profit. It does, however, raise serious questions about the social and personal benefits (or lack thereof) of technologies which encourage such a concentrated focus on the self.

In an age when individuality-on-steroids is presented as business as usual, the rise of digital technologies reflects and intensifies trends that have been knocking around Western culture for quite some time. Although the selfie is often uniquely linked with narcissism, it is difficult to say conclusively, based on the research currently available, that behaviours such as selfie-taking *cause* narcissism. What they seem to do, in some cases – again, based on the evidence currently available – is exacerbate tendencies that an individual may already have.[15] One small-scale study in 2018 showed a link between excessive posting of visual content to social media and a subsequent increase in narcissism.[16] Another study in 2021 of US college students found that those with low levels of narcissism tended to post as many selfies as those with higher levels.[17] There is in fact some evidence to suggest that selfie-taking by men may exhibit higher degrees of narcissistic tendencies than selfie-taking by women, an interesting finding that potentially rains on the parade of the kinds of popular discourse that portray narcissistic selfie-takers as silly, self-obsessed young women.[18] This kind of discourse, as researcher Anne Burns points out, is 'a cloaked expression of sexist attitudes' designed to 'not merely *express* prejudice toward others; it also *justifies* their denigration by establishing punishment as a socially accepted response to certain activities (taking selfies) and subjects (women who take selfies)' [emphasis Burns'].[19] So the next time you hear someone decrying the selfie as a sign of the rampant narcissism of feeble-minded millennials and Gen Z-ers – and by extension, signifying everything that is wrong with the modern world – perhaps take a moment to consider, if only for yourself, that the reality might be a lot more nuanced.

If an alien were to land from outer space and scan the media to figure out what a selfie is or does, they'd be highly flummoxed. Are selfies daring proclamations of self-love, igniting change-making levels of female empowerment with every pout and click? Or do they signal the end of Western civilisation, precipitated by a descent into bacchanalian levels of narcissism? Are selfies a way of telling radical truths about our lives or a means of spreading toxic fairy tales that make us feel like frauds? Are they photographs, or performances, or both? And if no one seems to be sure what the exact benefits of selfies are, then why do humans take so bloody many of them?

Although we talk about selfies as if they are entirely new, the reality is that people have long had the impulse to record their lives and leave their mark. Tens of thousands of years ago our ancient ancestors painted their handprints on the walls of caves, leaving vivid drawings we can still see today. Many centuries later, the wealthy and powerful (such as our pal King Ludwig I of Bavaria) were among the few who had the means to have artworks created, often in their likeness or in the likeness of those they loved or desired, which are now displayed in our museums and galleries. Although new in terms of technology, the selfie is in fact part of a long history of cultural practices stemming from the human desire for recognition; our need to be seen, however fleetingly; and the need to preserve the likeness of what we love. It is also part of the technological evolution of popular photography, a practice that became mainstream at the beginning of the twentieth century. Then, as now, companies needed to find consumers and markets for their new products. This led the once all-powerful Kodak company to develop their iconic Kodak Girl to sell their easy-to-use Brownie camera to female customers.[20] The Kodak Girl was fashionable, freedom-loving and unthreateningly attractive – not unlike the aspirational figure of the influencer today. It is ironic to note that, just over a hundred years after the launch of the Brownie, the arrival of Instagram – a start-up at the time with under twenty employees – helped put Kodak out of business in 2012.[21]

While the media likes to talk about the selfie in hyperbolic terms, the majority of the women I've spoken to over the course of my work exploring the phenomenon view it in ways that are ambivalent rather than blindly enthusiastic. Far from posing and snapping without a second thought, selfie use is something many selfie-takers think deeply about as they negotiate the tricky types of visibility social media both offers and demands. There is also a considerable financial commitment involved in producing the kinds of selfies that are a hit on sites such as Instagram. Taking a 'good' selfie requires resources (the money to buy a phone with a decent quality camera, for starters), skills in terms of styling and make-up, and the cultural nous to understand how to package the image to appeal to one's anticipated audience. Given the emotional and social stakes involved, this should come as no surprise, except perhaps for those who wrongly assume selfie-takers are somehow exceptionally deficient when it comes to self-awareness. Yet few cultural practices make us as hyper-aware of ourselves and of our physical shortcomings as the selfie, in which participants are invited to survey their appearance at a forensic level before submitting it for the eyes of others. It is a practice riddled with contradictions and tensions, where the desire to see idealised versions of one's self and to be seen by others on platforms primed for judgement produces a complex web of pleasure and vulnerability.

Part of the reason popular understandings of the selfie remain limited is that discussions about the phenomenon rarely centre the perspectives of those who take them, especially young women. This creates a whole lot of hot air but little in the way of insight. 'A lot of my selfies don't see the light of day – it's more like a personal diary,' Ciara, a writer like performer, tells me over email. 'In general, I'm a big fan of candid photos. I think they usually look more like the person than a selfie does.' In a few short sentences, Ciara, and many women I've spoken to over the years, complicates the idea that selfie-takers are simply rabid attention-seekers. On the contrary, people take selfies in different ways for different reasons in different contexts, and not all of them are to be shared. For Ciara, they act as a sort of journal. For others, as with traditional photography, it can be as simple as preserving a memory or a feeling or recording something they are proud about – hardly the stuff of pathological narcissism. Others take selfies because they feel that doing so is now a requirement of contemporary femininity. Like wearing make-up, getting one's hair done or being a certain body shape, for better or worse, many women feel that selfies are now expected of them.

In her email Ciara also hits on something I too have observed. Often a selfie has little to do with the actual self, either internal or external, particularly when it is intended for the likes of Instagram, where the selfies that get the greatest visibility generally follow a very specific blueprint. Taking their cues from the glossy aesthetics of stars such as the Kardashians (more of whom later), these types of selfie are usually devised in response to culturally prescribed notions of how a person should be, which are often at loggerheads with how the majority of us actually are. But it's not just about conformity; it's also about control. 'Selfies can be seen as an empowering way of capturing your image, a way that you have total control over,' Ciara writes in response to my asking about the good and bad aspects of the selfie. In an age when smartphones have made being photographed an everyday event rather than a special occasion, it is not surprising that the control selfies confer in terms of self-representation should be a big part of their appeal. Recalling a positive selfie experience, Ciara says:

> I remember when I first started growing out my armpit hair and decided to post a selfie showing it off. It's no big deal now, but at the time it felt so risky to show this non-conforming side of me. Once I posted it though, and people were reacting well, I felt really elated, and I really appreciated all the likes and comments. Funnily enough I met a girl years later who said she had stopped shaving after seeing the photo on my Instagram. So, I believe in the power of selfies to self-empower and to even empower others.

Here Ciara captures a major factor of the selfie's appeal: its representational power. Instead of being isolated by her rejection of beauty norms, or letting them be dictated to her through the pages of a magazine, the selfie enabled Ciara to find a supportive community that embraced rather than rejected her choice. This capacity for self-representation is particularly compelling for those who have been denied representation in traditional media and in the wider public sphere. Writing in *The Guardian* in 2015 in an article entitled 'Selfies allow black women to say we are here, and we are beautiful,' Syreeta McFadden outlines the way the selfie can be used to expand visual culture: 'While the mainstream may not yet reflect a wide, true and constructed representation of people of colour, we're creating space for that existence in the cyberworld. We're cultivating a vernacular to understand our images beyond stilted paradigms.'[22] McFadden's point is echoed in the work of academic Mehita Iqani who explores how female celebrities from the Global South use the selfie to challenge Eurocentric beauty norms on social media and beyond.[23] It echoes too in the work of those who refuse to make themselves invisible online, like British disability-rights campaigner Melissa Blake, who, when told by trolls she should refrain from posting images of herself on social media, published a defiant flurry of selfies in response.[24]

When used subversively and politically, selfies have the potential to disrupt the status quo and answer back to it, turning visibility into a political act. In 2014 the then Turkish Deputy Prime Minister Bülent Arinç declared that women should not laugh in public so as to stop 'moral corruption'. It appeared that for men like Arinç, women's laughter and their use of the selfie were uniquely threatening to the social order. Unimpressed but emboldened, Turkish women flocked to social media to post selfies of themselves laughing, using the hashtags #direnkahkaha (resist laughter) and #direnkadin (resist woman). The Turkish journalist Ece Temelkuran, who was one of the first women to post a picture in response to Arinç's controversial remarks, told the BBC, 'My whole timeline was full of women laughing, which was extraordinary, and kind of beautiful.'[25]

Selfie hashtag campaigns, especially those espousing 'empowerment' of various kinds, circulate all the time. From #nomakeupselfie to #Ilooklikeanengineer to #YesAllWomen, these campaigns generally serve a genuine, well-meaning purpose, often tied to highlighting inequalities that persist offline as much as online. Problems arise, however, when political intent is overshadowed by the self-branding practices that are social media's *lingua franca*, producing little in the way of material change but lots of good PR for those already in privileged positions. Escaping the limits of these practices – even for those with the best of intentions and the worthiest of causes – is not easy, since the attention online campaigns rely on depends on the visibility offered by social media. It controls the board, so if you want to play, you have to play by its rules and those rules tend to grant the most visibility to images of stereotypically attractive women with large platforms.

Case in point: in July 2020 the #ChallengeAccepted #WomenSupportingWomen hashtags produced a lot of very becoming black-and-white celebrity selfies and quite a few scratched heads. It wasn't clear what the stakes of the challenge were, what undertaking it involved or how exactly it supported women. Writing about the hashtags' nebulous origins and purpose, journalist Claire Lampen observed 'any original aims of the hashtag have now been obscured', adding that 'the social-justice message feels a little hollow when the main focus is on participants' flawless faces'.[26] As often is the case for these types of campaigns, while the #ChallengeAccepted #WomenSupportingWomen selfies used social media visibility to latch onto vaguely defined ideas of female empowerment, garnering lots of likes in the process and more exposure for some already very high-profile women, what they manifested in terms of tangible change at a moment of intense global suffering remains to be seen.

During the pandemic, while legacy media organisations floundered, social media engagement soared as people began to spend even more time online. The platform leading the field in this usership boom was the selfie's spiritual home, Instagram,[27] the site most associated with the phenomenon in popular consciousness. While Instagram is notable for the vibrant communities it fosters (see the glamorous older women of @advancedstyle or the Muslim artist collective @variantspaceart or the celebration of lesbian popular culture that is @butchcamp), it is also notorious for its promotion of conformity, especially when it comes to beauty standards. This perhaps should not be surprising given how intensely visual Instagram culture is.

Writing in *The Beauty Myth* in the early nineties, Naomi Wolf described how, in the aftermath of second-wave feminism, just as women in the West were gaining increased economic power and greater agency over their lives, images of beauty were being used to contain the threat this new independence symbolised to the status quo.[28] Central to this was a sexist and limiting cultural expectation that placed enormous emphasis on attractiveness, coercing women into a silent war against their own bodies. Wolf called this effect 'a political weapon against women's advancement', the defeat of which would require women to develop 'a new way to see'.[29]

Although Instagram enables women to self-represent, the degree to which this is producing new ways to see is debatable – particularly when it comes to the kinds of visibility that cannot be easily commodified and subsumed by consumerism, beyond the sort that slightly expand visual culture without fundamentally changing it. Because while platforms such as Instagram enable users to create images, this creating occurs within boundaries that are set by the technology, not the individual.

While researching this chapter, I downloaded the Facetune2 selfie-editing app which, at the time of writing, makes me of one more than 20 million people to do so since 2016. Was I seduced by the luminous version of myself that appeared after some 'light' editing? Naturally. Did this do anything to assuage my misgivings about the app's aims? Not in the slightest.

Just like advertising and the fashion–beauty complex[30] before it, apps like Facetune exist to profit off insecurities they create to exacerbate. The difference now is that this exacerbation is abetted by a culture where the expectation of being photographed or videoed during daily life and your image being subjected to public judgement has quickly become part of everyday life. This has specific resonances for women who have always been defined, as the feminist scholar Laura Mulvey put it, by their 'to-be-looked-at-ness'.[31] Add to this the generally accepted expectation that one should *want* to make oneself visible online – in the right way, of course. In short, these apps are being offered as salves for pressures stemming from the rising demand for visibility that they themselves represent. Today, thanks to ye gods of digital technology, not only do we take more photographs than ever before, but our photographs have never been so public or so scrutinised. With a multitude of ways to be seen, there are fewer and fewer places to hide from the spotlight of perpetual visibility. Yet we rarely ask ourselves *why* we accept this increasing surveillance and quantification of our lives. Instead, we rely on the features social media offers up to make the endless demand for visibility more palatable and manageable.

Despite my misgivings about Facetune, even I must admit that it boasts an impressive range of quick ways to 'perfect' your image, especially if you can afford a monthly subscription to 'unlock' its full array of self-editing tools. How Facetune describes the options it provides users is both fascinating and telling. Take, for example, options like 'Smooth', 'Heal' and 'Patch'. Note how they subtly suggest some form of unspecified but unseemly physical deficiency on behalf of the user. 'Smooth' your hairy / spotty / wrinkled (circle as appropriate) skin. 'Heal' the bits of you that are supposedly broken, otherwise what is there to 'heal'? 'Patch' sounds like a dressing for a wound. There's a cunning, unspoken binary at work on Planet Facetune (edited-self equals 'better', unedited-self equals 'yikes!'), which assumes that users' faces and bodies are inherently flawed entities that require fixing, which Facetune is conveniently on hand to do. Imagine that.

While they dangle the keys of aesthetic perfection, beauty apps and filters are designed to fragment bodies in intricate and minute ways, where seeing oneself through technology means carving up one's face into parts – nose, teeth, eyes, eyebrows, cheekbones and so forth – to be meticulously examined on our screens. This produces a strange effect where supposed 'defects' users didn't even know they had become not only identified but magnified. As a 'solution', software with the powerful capabilities of Photoshop – a programme that was until fairly recently far beyond the reach of mortals, reserved for fashion magazines and the advertising industry – can show users, in the space of a few quick clicks, how they would look if their nose were smaller or their teeth were whiter or if they lost ten pounds or had a thimble of Botox injected into their foreheads. It is seductive and fascinating, a handy, low-effort way to alleviate the pressure of having to be so visible all the time, but it can also be akin to taking an AK47 to your self-esteem.

In the same moment they grant us our desires, every filter we apply, every self- edit we make reminds us how we fail to measure up to what society deems beautiful. It teaches us that *to be seen* means that *we must conform*, even when we do not recognise the altered image staring back at us. The cruellest twist is how the apps and filters that cleverly offer themselves up as the solution to looking effortlessly perfect are themselves heavily invested in promoting the most dubious aspects of the beauty myth. As professor of digital culture Jill Walker Rettberg points out, technologies like filters are not simply technological – they are *cultural*, meaning they reflect the values of the societies from which they emerge.[32]

When societies have limiting expectations about what women should be and how they should look, it is no great surprise to see these demands baked into the technologies they produce, technologies which, far too often, are presented to users as neutral. Why is it, for example, that beauty apps and filters emphasise certain types of looks and not others? Why are they so obsessed with suggesting we erase the parts of ourselves that make us unique, that give us character, that speak to the identities and histories that make us who we are? Freckles: removed. Roman noses: vamoosed. Laughter lines: expunged. Skin tone: lightened or darkened, depending on the preferences of the culture. Is it coincidental, or is it a telling example of how society and the media grants elevated forms of visibility to certain types of femininity while ignoring or ridiculing others, producing a visual culture where only Barbie-esque levels of blandness and conformism are tolerated?

Beauty apps and filters work by directing users to see themselves and others through highly judgemental lenses. Learning to fragment ourselves into 'bits' to be edited and evaluated for Instagram likes, teaches us to view and experience our bodies as a series of deficiencies to be dissected, rather than what they are: a temple to human uniqueness and a miracle of evolution that keeps us alive. For decades, feminists have sounded the alarm on the dangers inherent to the fragmentation of women's bodies by advertising and media industries as a malign expression of the male gaze. Objectification (a term we do not use nearly enough these days) relies on the repeated and systematic breaking-down of women's bodies so they come to represent parts, not a person. In the age of social media, it is not only advertisers and the traditional media who engage in this practice: every day, users are encouraged to fragment and find fault with themselves and each other through the logic of apps whose entire business plan relies on offering solutions to the 'problems' they've helped create. This puts users at risk of internalising and projecting onto themselves cultural and technological gazes that are intensely critical, a process known as 'self-objectification'.

The normalisation and ubiquity of these kinds of selfie-practices should not be taken lightly. As the comedian Marcia

Belsky writes: 'The consistent fragmentation of women's bodies ... separates the sexualized female body parts from her wholeness. Thus, as fragmented parts, the viewer does not have to morally reconcile the woman who is being objectified with her complete humanness.'[33] This quote comes from the website of the 'Headless Women of Hollywood' project, created by Belsky. The project collects film posters, book covers and other promotional materials featuring the figure of the headless woman, of which there appears to be no end. As Belsky argues, the cumulative effect of this kind of imagery is alarming. With fragmentation comes dehumanisation and alienation; but this process has never been just about selling products. It is also about selling a vision of reality. As one of the pioneers of media-literacy education Jean Kilbourne puts it, 'Ads sell more than products ... They sell concepts of normalcy ... They tell us who we are and who we should want to be.'[34]

Like the advertising industry, beauty apps push standardised ideas of beauty, making them a powerful lens through which users see and, most importantly, critique themselves and each other. This is not only an individualising process; it is an isolating one in which people's appearances – our own included – become entities to be endlessly monitored, ranked and appraised, spreading competitiveness like a toxin. This gaze incorporates elements of the male gaze but it also encourages a distinct form of a hypercritical female gaze through which women learn to look at themselves and each other in ways that are disciplining rather than pleasurable. These dynamics are further intensified by social media's endless enticements to judge – like this, retweet that, leave a comment or don't (letting silence send a nasty message) – through which users are encouraged to seek validation for themselves and grant it (or not) to others.

The more we invest of ourselves in these technologies, the greater they shape way the way we see ourselves and the way we see others. A creeping, uneasy awareness of being looked at by audiences known and unknown becomes part of daily life. As writer Tavi Gevinson said of her reliance on social media during a key period of her career, 'With Instagram, self-defining and self-worth measuring spilled over into the rest of the day, becoming my default mode.'[35] This produces an effect where, for all the babble about empowering people to 'be themselves', the visibility offered by platforms like Instagram inevitably veers towards the conformist and the performative. But this is not only about social media turning us into boring, obedient avatars; it is also about the toll the fragmentation between self and image extracts on women's minds and bodies.

Whether you are a regular selfie-taker or not, if you are a frequent social media user, you are probably spending a lot of time navigating the intensely visual, judgemental online world from whence they spring. Understanding this selfie-centred landscape and its impact on users is something researchers across multiple fields are working on but the insights here are drawn from psychology and behavioural science. Although much more remains to be done in this relatively new and rapidly evolving area, these findings are valuable, particularly when it comes to understanding how these activities impact a user's sense of self. Often, these studies confirm the deep ambivalence that surrounds practices like the selfie, an ambivalence that tends to veer towards the negative rather than the positive.

While much is made of the pleasure and empowerment that women derive from posting selfies, the findings of a 2018 study published in *Body Image* gives pause for thought. This is not least because it is the first study of its kind to show that taking and posting selfies on social media can cause adverse psychological effects for women.[36] Compared to a control group who did not post selfies, researchers found that women who did, 'reported feeling more anxious, less confident, and less physically attractive afterwards'.[37] Researchers also found the ability to retake and edit their images did not assuage these feelings. In another study, taking and editing selfies was shown to produce 'increased negative mood and facial dissatisfaction', with greater self-editing indicating a deeper sense of dissatisfaction. The researchers concluded that 'investing heavily in editing one's self-presentation on social media is a detrimental activity for young women'.[38] This investment has also been shown to negatively impact women's body image and stimulate a desire for thinness that can lead to disordered eating.[39] With these findings in mind, if you are the type of person who posts a selfie when feeling low in the hope of being cheered up by positive responses, or uses social media to get the approval you feel you need, it is worth considering if these practices are truly serving you or if they are doing more harm than good.

Where and how we post also matters. Researchers found that users posting selfies to Instagram experienced a greater degree of self-scrutiny and comparison compared to posting on Facebook, a platform that places less of an emphasis on images.[40] Rather than general social media use, findings also suggest that 'selfie' activities, particularly those that orientate around beauty practices, are especially associated with lower body satisfaction and a desire for thinness.[41] Taken together, these findings indicate that being mindful of what platforms we use and how we use them is critical to tracing the connection between social media use and our sense of self. This is underscored in a 2019 study that linked self-objectification via selfie-taking to depression, leading the authors to caution 'how one uses social media matters'.[42]

The types of selfie imagery to which we expose ourselves also appears to matter. Researchers have found that viewing no-make-up selfies, compared to highly idealised images of attractive women, did not negatively impact women's mood and body image.[43] Fitspiration images, on the other hand, caused higher levels of body dissatisfaction and negative mood compared to viewing travel images.[44] Humour, it seems, also plays an interesting role. Exposure to accounts parodying celebrity selfie culture (see Celeste Barber's hugely popular Instagram)[45] and those contrasting unedited images with their retouched counterparts (see Reddit's Instagram versus reality subreddit, aka Instagram Reality Baybeh!)[46] produced increased body satisfaction and positive mood.[47] Laughter is good medicine and while more research is needed, these early findings suggest that curating what we expose ourselves to online can help protect against the negative emotional impacts of selfie culture.

In January 2019 the acclaimed British fashion photographer Rankin conducted an Instagram experiment with a group of teenagers. After taking a headshot of each, he asked them to edit their image until they were happy with it, using techniques that have become synonymous with the selfie. He posted his shocked reaction to the outcome on his Instagram account:[48] 'I photographed teenagers & handed them the image to then edit & filter until they felt the image was "social media ready". People are mimicking their idols, making their eyes bigger, their nose smaller and their skin brighter, and all for social media likes.' Calling on people to 'acknowledge the damaging effects that social media has on people's self-image', he concluded that this process was one of the reasons why 'we are living in a world of FOMO, sadness, increased anxiety, and Snapchat dysmorphia'.[49]

It's easy to be a cynical about Rankin's alarm. Here, after all, is someone who made his name working in fashion, an industry amongst the guiltiest when it comes to stimulating feelings of inadequacy to swell their coffers. Another way to look at it is that Rankin's immersion in the fashion–beauty vortex puts him in a unique position when it comes to spotting what is new, and uniquely troubling, about the kinds of self-editing sites like Instagram and apps like Facetune encourage. While social media's links to rising levels of anxiety, depression and cosmetic surgery should not be put down to simplistic, monocausal notions of cause and effect – social phenomena, like people, are more complex than that and more research into the interconnectedness of these issues is needed – something is shifting in terms of how we see ourselves, and not necessarily for the better. This is reflected in the rise of terms such as those Rankin mentioned such as 'Snapchat dysmorphia' and 'selfie dysmorphia'. These stem from plastic surgeons' accounts of patients bringing their selfies to consultations instead of the usual celebrity pictures. In a *VICE* video report entitled 'I Got Surgery to Look Like my Snapchat and Facetune Selfie,'[50] one of the young women interviewed describes Facetune as 'plastic surgery on your phone'. She rationalises her desire for a nose job saying, 'I might as well get the real surgery to become the image that I really want to portray.' Like Essena O'Neill, seeing herself through technology has produced an uncomfortable sense of distance between her actual self and her selfie, a distance she is willing to pay a considerable amount of money in the hope of bridging.

Although simplistic explanations for the appeal of the selfie proliferate today as much as they did in 2013 when the word first entered the Oxford English Dictionary, it is a phenomenon that defies basic explanations. As we've seen throughout this chapter, the selfie is fuelled by instincts as old as humanity itself, channelled through a mix of historical and technological legacies to the cultural upheaval of the present. As a form of self-representation, selfies have a natural resonance for those for whom seeing themselves as they wish to be seen is still a struggle. For those who believe in the power of self-branding, they can be a handy tool to show others the self you want them to see, however accurate that image may or may not be. For women, who for so long have been the object of the gaze rather than its subject, selfies are a way to assert one's perspective and create a different type of visual culture.

But selfies are also bound to commercial platforms that are designed to commodify and standardise visibility, where algorithms prioritise the conventional and where enticements to judge transform the pleasure of looking at oneself and others into communal surveillance. Platforms such as Instagram can help build communities, but can also destroy them through the emphasis they put on individual status, judgement and competitiveness. These platforms can provide the space to challenge stereotypes and inequalities while also being predisposed to reproduce them. They can instil deep feelings of personal empowerment that can quickly mutate into self-doubt and distraction while doing little to advance equality in a broad sense. As Syreeta McFadden writes of selfies, 'there are limits to self-love before it morphs into self-absorption or worse'.[51]

In 2019, after a four-year break, Essena O'Neill returned to the internet. In an interview[52] about her new website venture, O'Neill described the financial and emotional hardships she endured as an influencer and in the aftermath of the very public abdication of her once high-profile career, saying, 'I've been working many shitty jobs. I've been struggling. It hasn't been great.' Asked why she has chosen to return to the world that once caused her so much pain, O'Neill describes how she misses the connections with like-minded people that the internet can foster but that this time around she is doing things very differently: her website, Authority Within, makes it clear how differently.[53] In a section entitled 'Neoliberal Royalty' (illustrated with a photo of the Kardashians), O'Neill writes, 'Safe to say our celebrity culture is peak evidence of our servitude to artificial beauty and endless material consumption? Cause damn don't those in power *always* look their best ... are we living in some weird Emperor's New Clothes post-capitalist bullshit future? [emphasis O'Neill's]'

Scrolling through a section entitled 'Alienation' brings up quotes from writers James Baldwin and Victor Hugo on the impact of poverty, and George Orwell on surveillance. It also links to a documentary series by Adam Curtis called *The Century of the Self*, which looks at how propaganda tools developed in Europe during World War Two were later used in public relations and advertising to create the West's consumer culture, where image-driven desire rather than basic needs became the key motivator of people's shopping habits and their sense of self.

At the time of writing O'Neill does have an Instagram account,[54] although there are only two posts on it. One says: 'Social media is my platform, not my life.' The other: 'I like the real you more than I like the Instagram you.' Neither one of the images is a selfie.

Three

Bodies

In 2013 Canadian artist and photographer Petra Collins penned a widely shared personal essay expressing her anger at Instagram's decision to terminate her account. Writing in *The Huffington Post*, Collins protested that she had done nothing to violate the site's terms of use.[1] What she had done, she said, was to dare to post a picture that didn't conform to cultural ideals of how a feminine body should look. The image in question was a medium close-up of Collins' pale torso, clad in light-blue bikini briefs, against a sparkling backdrop. On a platform that features no end of revealing clothing, it was, in the main, an unremarkable image. But Collins' shot contained one thing that, while entirely natural, is usually absent in this kind of imagery: her pubic hair. By including it, Collins sparked one of the first of many high-profile examples of how tightly Instagram governs visibility on its platform.

By showing what Collins described as 'my own unaltered state – an unshaven bikini line',[2] she triggered the powerful but opaque tripwire that this chapter explores: the moderation codes and algorithmic biases that determine who gets to be seen on Instagram, and the contradictions and inconsistencies they produce. Because while self-representation on social media draws on language that sees such activities as a channel for change, creativity and self-expression, the type of visibility offered by Instagram is often conformist rather than transformative, especially when it comes to representations of the body. It also raises questions about transparency and ideology on platforms that present themselves as 'neutral', where the rules that govern visibility are at once unclear to users but are also informed by stereotypes and commercial concerns that tend to reproduce rather than resist inequality.

In her essay, Collins connects her experience to a wider societal distrust and disgust for non-airbrushed and otherwise non-confirming feminine bodies.[3] This produces a double standard that prevails on digital platforms as much as it does in older forms of media. Nowhere is this clearer on social media than in Instagram's infamous 'nipple policy', where the female nipple is banned but male nipples are permitted. Since one nipple is much the same as the next nipple (see the @genderless_nipples Instagram account for proof, if needed), one can only conclude that this rule reflects cultural meanings society projects onto feminine bodies rather than women's nipples being uniquely dangerous.

For Collins, the internet had once seemed to provide her with a space apart from sexist visual culture; somewhere she could connect with other young women who shared her desire to, as she writes, 'strive to change the way we look and treat ourselves'.[4] But the criticism her image provoked, along with the censoring of her account, brought the preoccupations of the offline world crashing in.

Instagram's response to Collins' attempt to represent her body outside prescribed notions of beauty revealed how deeply cultural ideas can influence how we see through digital technology and how, in turn, the technology 'sees' us. A smattering of pubic hair – for that is all Collins' photograph showed – poses no threat to anyone, other than perhaps to those whose experience of feminine bodies is limited to highly edited, pornified images or those who find such bodies inherently 'dirty'. If the issue is genuinely about potential harm, one is inclined to wonder how much of a threat an untrimmed bikini line is on a platform that is also home to accounts like @firearms, which boasts 2.1 million followers for showcasing 'The Best Guns on Instagram'. As a defiant Collins argued in her essay, rather than projecting regressive attitudes onto her image, those standing in judgement would do well to question where their discomfort comes from and ask why a natural, unedited body should provoke them so.

Collins' attempt to use social media to expand how women's bodies are represented met with the kinds of disapproving surveillance and intense criticism that have long sought to reassert 'normal' ideas of how a woman's body should look. The irony, of course, is that Collins' shot captures an actual facet of the body that is routinely removed from so-called 'normal' images, especially those that are sexualised. Using technological tools of self-representation, she created a subversive image and a political one. It is an image that contrasts sharply with the unreality of many bodies on Instagram and in the media more broadly; bodies that have been Photoshopped, carefully posed and surgically enhanced. Yet, like Lauren Miranda's selfie, this image was interpreted by those who complained about it as shameful and disgusting. These complaints were then legitimised by Instagram through its deletion of Collins' account as if Collins' image and its intent were the problem.

During a period when women's empowerment has become synonymous with social media use, Collins and Miranda both used digital technology to express themselves, exploring sexuality and femininity through a distinctly female gaze. But in doing so they were disciplined through that very same technology. For all their agency and intent, the photos they produced could not escape dominant interpretations that regarded their images as unacceptable, and their behaviour as punishable. While social media is still relatively new, it draws heavily on the visual cultures of film, photography, art and advertising, which, until quite recently, promoted limiting ideas of what a woman's body should look like and who it should exist for; where the only feminine bodies fit for public recognition are those of Victoria's Secret models – lithe, oiled and hairless, glistening with sexuality but primed solely for a heterosexual male gaze. In Collins' case, her attempt to claim visibility while expanding what is visually acceptable led to a complete denial of her visibility on Instagram, an experience she describes as, 'like a physical act, like the public coming at me with a razor, sticking their finger down my throat, forcing me to cover up, forcing me to succumb to society's image of beauty'.[5]

On the 'About' page on Instagram's website, users are invited to 'express yourself', 'stand out on Instagram' and 'build influence' by creating 'compelling content that's distinctly yours'.[6] This paean to the joys of individuality is very much at odds with experiences like Collins', where, in trying to be distinctive by creating content that provokes much-needed questioning of what visual culture considers 'normal', users face discipline and censorship. Feminists have long criticised the way traditional media sanitises and polices the realities of women's bodies, from ads for sanitary towels using that strange blue liquid in lieu of anything vaguely red, to the still-stifling homogeneity of much fashion and beauty imagery, to monitoring celebrities' post-pregnancy figures to see how quickly they 'pop' back into shape. Feminists have also criticised how exclusionary such imagery is, ignoring the rich diversity of women's identities and experiences. In theory, sites like Instagram have the potential to expand visual culture and knock limiting representations on their head, given how they enable women to take their own pictures and tell their own stories. But right from Instagram's ascent in the early 2010s, when users attempted to do so using images of cellulite, mastectomies, period blood, pregnancy, body hair, nipples, gender diverse and gender non-conforming bodies and desires beyond the heterosexual, they quickly came up against the limits of this supposedly pro-self-expression space.

In just a decade Instagram has not only changed visual culture; increasingly, it defines it, shaping the 'look' of everything from clothing to interiors to holidays. While the women's magazine market is in freefall, a trend exacerbated by the pandemic, the content it helped pioneer flourishes anew on Instagram where advertisers can reach global audiences and customers can shop from their beds by simply clicking a link. Now, rather than seeking guidance and a sense of community through the pages of *Glamour* or *Marie Claire* (two examples of the many magazines that have expanded their online presence and reduced their print offerings in recent years while many others have ceased publication for good), women increasingly turn to the internet and the connections it fosters. As digital content can be discussed, liked and shared with immediacy, it engages the reader in ways the humble page cannot. Yet with some exceptions, Instagram culture largely remains as standardised as it is in the magazines it migrated from, particularly when it comes to those with the most followers and the highest level of visibility. As internet researcher Alice Marwick points out, while diversity certainly exists on the platform, in the main users tend to reproduce 'very conventional beauty standards and aesthetics'.[7]

Instagram's association with feminine culture, particularly the diet, beauty, lifestyle and fashion industries, is borne out in its usership stats. According to a 2017 report by Instagram planning and scheduling tool Hopper, there are slightly more women than men on Instagram, with women receiving on average five times the likes that men do.[8] Men are also ten times more likely to comment on a post by a woman than on a post by another man.[9] In terms of engagement then, content created by women and their presence on the site is a core aspect of what drives Instagram's metrics. Yet issues with harassment and visibility (who gets to be seen, who does not and the costs of this in/visibility) persist. As just one example, in 2019 Australian researchers described how female Instagram influencers felt that they had no choice but to tolerate abusive comments left on the site or risk damaging their brand. Writing about their study and its subjects, the researchers noted that for these women, 'reading such harassment, and making the choice to not delete it, simply becomes "part of the job".'[10]

This prevalence of a disciplining male gaze can be found in the judgements hurled by other users at Collins' image – 'disgusting', 'shameful', etc. etc. etc. – and by Instagram itself in its revoking of her account, a move that could easily be read as a form of punishment for her nonconformity.

After all, there are millions of images of women wearing briefs or bikini bottoms circulating on Instagram, often in a highly sexualised manner. The question is not what Collins wore but how she wore it, at the root of which is her refusal to self-edit her body hair against a culture that demands women be visible but only in the right way. As Laura Mulvey outlined in her landmark essay on the male gaze,[11] this type of gaze is fascinated by women yet longs to control them, creating on-screen images of objectified feminine characters who represent a safe but sexual spectacle for the male characters and the audience. This requires that all the messy realities of actual bodies be removed from sight – the blood, the body hair, the fat, the wrinkles, the personality and intellect animating it – so that all that remains is a smooth, 'clean', svelte and above all pliant archetype.

For centuries the majority of the feminine bodies circulating in popular Western culture were created by men, for men. Even when directed at women, these images conformed to traditional notions of femininity, which women were expected to embody through consumption and grooming. In a short space of time social media has turned this model on its head, but as cases like Petra Collins' make clear, this is not necessarily as progressive or stereotype-shattering as it first appears. Because while Instagram trades on users' desire to see and be seen, it also draws on and perpetuates a visual culture laden with sexist expectations, hierarchies of gender, race, class, ability and sexuality, and other questionable norms. As philosopher Susan Bordo wrote, 'images are never "just" pictures',[12] highlighting how powerfully visual culture shapes our understanding of ourselves and the world around us, helping to form the basis of what a society considers 'normal'. As the largest single repository of photographic images the world has ever known, Instagram is about much more than 'just' seeing and being seen. Pleasurable, influential and challenging, it captures one of the visibility trap's core conundrums: how platforms that offer women tools for self-representation embolden cultural forces intent on dictating how – and even if – they can access this new visibility.

In the summer of 2020, the black British model and body-positivity activist Nyome Nicholas-Williams had a series of portraits taken by photographer Alexandra Cameron. According to *The Observer*, the style of the shoot was one designed by Cameron for her customers to help boost women's self-esteem in what she called a 'confidence shoot'.[13] It didn't take long for Cameron to take an image with which she was delighted. Just fifteen minutes in, she used natural light to snap a topless Nicholas-Williams sitting on a stool with one arm around her breasts, eyes lowered as if in contemplation. An intimate image that is striking for its lack of artifice on a platform renowned for its artificiality, the shot invited the viewer in while centring Nicholas-Williams' quiet self-acceptance.[14] Covering her breasts with her arms, allowing no hint of the dreaded female nipple, Nicholas-Williams' pose reflected thousands of similar images posted to Instagram every day, most of which are not judged to have broken the platform's rules on nudity.

Nicholas-Williams explained to *The Observer* that when she posted the image on her Instagram account, the response from her followers was immediately enthusiastic. But just a few hours later the shot disappeared, along with others from the shoot, and Instagram had issued a threat to close her account. An upset Nicholas-Williams told the paper, 'Millions of pictures of very naked, skinny white women can be found on Instagram every day … But a fat black woman celebrating her body is banned? It was shocking to me. I feel like I'm being silenced.'[15] Cameron also expressed her frustration with the image's removal. She said that as a photographer she had never experienced this before, despite posting many images of white women wearing less clothing than Nyome – but these images had not been censored. Cameron added, 'What is it about a plus-size black woman's body that is so offensive and so sexualised? The *Playboy* feed is filled with naked white models and it's all for the male gaze, which is the opposite of what I do, and they're allowed to stay.'[16] That Nicholas-Williams' image was removed just two months after Instagram head Adam Mosseri tweeted, 'we're committed to looking at the ways our policies, tools, and processes impact black people and other under-represented groups on Instagram'[17] in response to the Black Lives Matter movement made the inconsistencies at play all the more glaring.

In contrasting Instagram's treatment of skinny white bodies with plus-size black ones, Nicholas-Williams and Cameron hit on a racial dynamic that has a long history in Western visual culture and today finds a new expression online. In her essay 'Selling Hot Pussy: Representations of Black Female Sexuality in the Cultural Marketplace', bell hooks describes how ideas of deviancy and hypersexuality assigned to black women's bodies under slavery continue to circulate in contemporary media.[18] Although writing before the arrival of social media, hooks' insights can still help us to pick apart the contradictory treatment of Nicholas-Williams' image compared to her slim Caucasian peers. Around the same time that the controversy over Nicholas-Williams' image erupted, Kylie Jenner posted a topless black-and-white photograph, covering her bare breasts with her arms, a pose not unlike Nicholas-Williams' but far more provocative.[19] This image was not removed, nor did it generate controversy, again underscoring the question of why Nicholas-Williams' image was censored.

It is also important to note that the Kardashians are regularly criticised for exploiting the very stereotypes hooks identifies, profiting from them to shore up their vast wealth while also reaping the benefits of whiteness and the power of the immense visibility they enjoy across numerous social media platforms, particularly Instagram.[20] A striking example of this was Kim Kardashian's 2014 tongue-in-cheek attempt to 'break the internet' using a nude image of herself shot from behind that clearly drew on the iconography of the Venus Hottentot.[21] The so-called 'Hottentot' – whose real name was Sarah Baartman – was a young woman brought to Paris from South Africa in the early nineteenth century. Baartman's naked body was turned into a voyeuristic display for French scientists and society because of its 'unusual' (by European standards) proportions. This was due to 'steatopygia', a build-up of fat around the buttocks and thighs common in women from sub-Saharan Africa.[22] Baartman died in poverty in Paris in 1815, aged twenty-six.[23] A cast of her body and skeleton continued to be displayed in France until the seventies.[24] On Instagram and elsewhere Kim Kardashian can playfully draw on this cruel legacy of objectification without fear of censure or invisibility. On the contrary: she can profit from it. Yet it is Nicholas-Williams, using social media and the female gaze to create images that challenge stereotypes of black bodies and plus-size bodies to create a different kind of visual language, who had her image disappeared into the digital ether.

Nicholas-Williams' experience shows how the motifs bell hooks critiqued back in the eighties – which, in turn, have their origins in the eighteenth and nineteenth century – continue to shape women's visibility today. We know what happened to Nicholas-Williams' image because it occurred on the front end of Instagram, the part users can engage with and see. This meant that it was clear to spot when Instagram removed the image; in this instance, people were aware of how the platform was trying to shape what they see and an outcry ensued, due in no small part to Nicholas-Williams' refusal to be rendered invisible or silent.

But the decision to remove Nicholas-Williams' image was made by mechanics that are hidden from view. The truth is, a great deal of what we see online is shaped by forces normal users cannot lay their eyes on, although we are becoming increasingly aware of their presence. What most of users think of as social media or the internet is only the tip of a large and complex technological iceberg,[25] most of which is submerged out of sight in the back end of devices and platforms and the vast network they are plugged into. So let's take a look under the bonnet of two of the most powerful, largely invisible forces governing what we see on social media: algorithms and moderators.

Writing in her 2018 book *Algorithms of Oppression: How Search Engines Reinforce Racism*,[26] Safiya Umoja Noble argues that the mathematical equations that help make social media so distracting and online advertising so targeted are also replicating social inequality. Noble's work is inspired by personal experience. The African American professor, when searching Google for content that might be of interest to her stepdaughters and nieces, was horrified by the results, the first hit being HotBlackPussy.com. As she and others[27, 28] researching algorithmic biases warn, far from being benign, objective forces that innocently optimise the user experience, algorithms, steeped in the biases of the humans who created them, can intensify marginalisation, reproducing exactly the kinds of racist and sexist tropes bell hooks warned about. Noble argues that rather than presuming what we see online to be 'truthful' or 'natural', users should instead be aware of how platforms – in this case Google's search engine – can 'perpetuate particular narratives' that 'reflect historically uneven distributions of power in society'.[29]

While Nicholas-Williams' experience took place on Instagram, the broader principle described by Noble still applies. All too often, when deciding who gets the greatest degree of visibility on their platforms, social media companies rely on moderation approaches that privilege content created by the Kardashians of the world. In doing so they reproduce harmful cultural ideas while sidelining those trying to do visibility differently. How social media companies do this can be difficult to unpack. There is little transparency about how algorithms are programmed, meaning that users can't generally know how – in mathematical or engineering terms – categories such as 'race' and 'gender' are determined, only that they are.[30] Like the moderation standards set out in Instagram's terms of use, algorithms are always in flux. Where moderation is carried out by humans, it is often in pressurised, time-sensitive environments in which individuals are expected to make fast judgements based on criteria set by social media companies. This can leave little scope or time for interpreting nuance or the creator's intent, or for interrogating one's own biases. The well-being of moderators should also give us pause for thought. More and more of them are now speaking out about what they say are the severe psychological and emotional effects of this work, which sees them exposed to reams of horrendous material every day with little support.[31]

These systems and their shadowy machinations have a major impact on user experience, as evidenced by the outcry in 2016 when Instagram changed from a chronologically ordered timeline to one determined by algorithm.[32] Two years later Instagram gave tech reporters a broad sketch of how its algorithm works, revealing the three core criteria shaping what users see in their feed: interest, based on what they have previously looked at; recency, based on the newness of the content; and relationship, based on the relationship between the user and those posting content.[33] The algorithm makes complex determinations about all these things, also considering how often a user logs in to Instagram, how long they spend on the app and how many accounts they follow. So while user feeds might seem like a natural manifestation of one's interests and interactions – after all, social media is designed to feel frictionless – in reality they are the result of an intricate weighing mechanism that determines what we see; mechanisms the average user has little control over.

Neither Nicholas-Williams nor her followers were willing to quietly accept Instagram's decision to remove her image. While she launched a highly publicised campaign against Instagram censorship, her followers kept reposting her images using the hashtag #IWantToSeeNyome until they were finally reinstated. When contacted by *Cosmopolitan* UK about the incident,[34] a Facebook spokesperson (remember, Facebook owns Instagram) pointed to the difficulties of moderating content for users as young as thirteen and a diverse global community: 'This can be a hard balance to strike, and that means there are times when our policies fall short. We don't allow breast squeezing as it is often associated with pornographic content, but we know we've made mistakes in how this has been enforced.' To address experiences like those of Nicholas-Williams', the spokesperson said moderators had been given 'new guidance' on distinguishing between 'squeezing breasts and simply holding or covering them'. They added, referring to the body positivity movement, 'We celebrate this community on Instagram and it is never our intention to silence their voices or bodies.' Alas, as Nicholas-Williams' story shows, good intentions alone are not enough to stop algorithmic and moderation overreach.

Removing images is one way Instagram controls visibility on its platform but it is not the only way. Case in point: the rise of what is colloquially referred to as 'shadow banning', where the visibility of a user's content mysteriously takes a nosedive. While images are not removed or banned outright, their ability to circulate and be seen is curtailed, a process that reminds creators in no uncertain terms just how much power Instagram has over their content. The murkiness of this arrangement was captured by a 2019 *Techcrunch* article,[35] which reported that Instagram, along with its owner Facebook, had begun to reduce the visibility of what it termed 'borderline content'. This referred to images and other material deemed to have come close to violating Community Standards on grounds such as nudity and violence. Facebook's rationale was that because extreme content tends to garner a greater degree of engagement it thus also achieves a greater degree of visibility. By reducing the visibility of content that it judges to be excessive but not rule-breaking, Facebook said it was attempting to counter-balance this effect.[36]

For many users outside the mainstream who rely on Instagram visibility for their work and to find like-minded people, these changes produced effects that were less than welcome. 'Finding a community of pole dancers on Instagram was very inspiring because you could see all sorts of bodies,' Dr Carolina Are tells me over Skype. She is a researcher, pole-dance instructor and blogger (bloggeronpole.com); she is also a member of the team of activists behind the EveryBODYVisible campaign. 'You could see plus-sized bodies, you could see LGBTQIA bodies, bodies with disabilities, with scars, what [in] normal society you would call "imperfections".' Carolina explains how she found healing through dance after suffering an abusive relationship and sexual assault: 'I didn't really see myself as having agency in my own body [...] my body was something that happened to me and it wasn't something that I took ownership of. So partly through pole dancing, but also partly through finding this community of pole dancers through Instagram, I could share my journey.'

In mid-2019, just a few months after the publication of the *Techcrunch* article on borderline content, Carolina noticed something strange going on with her Instagram. Content that had been popular seemed to be losing visibility. This was surprising. She was sure her posts had become better over time, thanks to her taking professional dance classes and using a better-quality camera to record her videos, so why was engagement dropping? 'If I looked for hashtag 'pole dance' or hashtag 'pole-dance nation' or whatever, which is also the name of a very popular account, [I] couldn't find anything,' she says. 'It would say "posts using this hashtag have been removed because they're against community guidelines".' Carolina points out that her community was not the only one affected: 'This censorship didn't only involve pole dancers; it involved erotic artists, artists, illustrators, photographers, models, athletes, LBGTQIA people, a lot of black people and lots of plus-sized activists.'

Carolina got in in touch with Instagram via their press office asking questions about what was happening to her content and that of others in her community. Meanwhile, pole dancers from all over the world started a petition calling on Instagram to 'please stop censoring pole dance', which quickly racked up almost twenty thousand signatures.[37] 'Those people noticed that I was writing blog posts [on the issue] and they noticed that I had that communication with Instagram, following that we all became a network,' Carolina explains, leading to the collaboration that would eventually become the EveryBODYVisible campaign:

> We all asked our networks what it was that they wanted to know about how Instagram was moderating pole dance. I went back to Instagram with those questions. They answered them, but for the first time ever, they gave me a direct quote apologising to pole dancers for moderating hashtags in error.[38] That was a big victory. I mean, it didn't make any difference. They stopped the censorship of those specific hashtags, but censorship still happened. But it was interesting to see that they admitted that they were wrong. After that, we were like, we don't want to stop here.

On 29 October 2019, International Internet Day, Carolina and her fellow activists launched EveryBODYVisible in response to repeated cases of shadow banning, encouraging consumers to flood social media with the hashtag #everybodyvisible and their own censorship stories. A statement on the campaign's website addressed the powers that be in Instagram/Facebook:

> We want to know, why is it okay to see people killing each other, but the body in its natural form is banned? Why is it okay to see one set of couples love each other but not another? Why is it okay to show female celebrities nude but not your average woman? We are determined for our message to be heard. It's simple … Let us be seen. Let us have the same space as everyone else. Social media, take responsibility with the power you have.[39]

Carolina explained that transparency around how Instagram grants and denies visibility was a key campaign demand. 'We were asking, "Tell us how your algorithms work. Who are your moderators, what are your policies?"' Despite the backlash their approach to borderline content provoked, in February 2020 Instagram head Adam Mosseri insisted that 'shadow banning is not a thing'.[40] For Carolina and her community and their many allies across diverse communities on Instagram, their experience suggests a different story.

In the summer of 2020 a televised ad for tampons featuring the catchphrase 'Get 'em up there girls!' caused huge controversy in Ireland. The ad was part of a campaign by Tampax called 'Tampons & Tea' designed to educate users on the correct way to insert a tampon after the company's survey of customers in the UK revealed that 79 per cent regularly or occasionally experienced discomfort.[41] A spokesperson for Tampax explained, 'we believe in normalising the conversation around periods through awareness, information and education … The light-hearted advert had centred around a very common usage question and the intent was to educate people on how to use the product.'[42] Not everyone in Ireland was convinced by this rationale. One critic called the ad 'offensive, crude, vulgar, disgusting, unnecessary, embarrassing, distasteful, coarse, grotesque, inappropriate and overdescriptive'.[43] In response to the outcry – although Ireland's Advertising Standards Authority described the ad as 'light-hearted', 'factual' and 'neither explicit nor graphic' – it ultimately decided to ban it for breaching its code by causing 'widespread offence'.[44]

The 'Tampons & Tea' approach to periods – frank, funny, grounded in real experience – was clearly not for everyone but its quest to normalise periods was a noble one. While Tampax's aim as a company is to drive sales, their interest in increasing awareness and information around periods dovetails with those campaigning for better menstrual education, the eradication of period stigma and those fighting period poverty to ensure the ready availability of sanitary products for whoever needs them. These issues affect billions of women and girls across the world every day. Research in the United States in 2019 found that period poverty was a leading cause for girls skipping school or not wanting to attend class while menstruating if they cannot access feminine hygiene products.[45] Of the 1000 teenagers surveyed, 64 per cent believe society teaches people to be ashamed of their periods, 66 per cent do not want to be at school while menstruating, while 80 per cent feel there is a negative association with periods, that they are 'gross' or 'unsanitary'.[46] No one should have to face into an emotional minefield like this every month, but that is what is happening, with potentially devastating long-term effects on girls' education. Just as poverty can prohibit access to sanitary products, so too can stigma and shame, making it difficult for adolescents to get the support and information they need for what is a basic fact of life.

That periods remain so cloaked in opprobrium in the twenty-first century – when women's bodies have never been so visible – is typical of the dissonance between fantasy women and their flesh-and-blood counterparts that has long been a hallmark of Western culture. One would think that digital technologies' new tools of self-representation would help change all that, letting women finally tell the story of their embodied selves in all its glorious, bloody detail. The reality, on social media at least, is not so simple.

In 2015 the then-student and now bestselling poet Rupi Kaur decided to put her photography project exploring menstrual taboos on her Instagram.[47] Like Collins' image, Kaur adopted a stripped-back, realistic aesthetic that eschewed anything filtered to perfection. One of her photos shows Kaur's bare feet in the shower with what appears to be her blood splattering the white tiles around the plughole. Another shows Kaur lying on a sofa in grey sweatpants and a white T-shirt, a pink hot water bottle clutched to her stomach, a position familiar to anyone who has ever suffered period cramps. The next shows her on the loo, grey sweatpants and underwear around her ankles, dropping a used sanitary towel into the bin. Its wrapper lies to the forefront of the image. Again, it is a shot that is on the one hand entirely mundane for half of humanity and on the other, unusual for its depiction of a reality that is rarely represented in mainstream visual culture.

Kaur's fourth image is the one that ignited the most controversy. Like the other photos in the series, it is shot in a simple, unadorned style using what appears to be grainy daylight. Kaur lies on her bed with her back to the camera, revealing a dark trail of blood staining the rump of her sweatpants and the sheets. Like the shower tiles, bathroom bin and hot-water bottle, the stains on Kaur's clothes and sheets make visible experiences that are routinely made invisible, experiences that are normal but are rarely represented as such. Her images are devoid of the tired and tin-eared 'go girl!' cheerfulness that is characteristic of so much tampon and sanitary-pad advertising, as if menstruating is another thing about which a woman is required to be effortless and ebullient.

Instead, Kaur captures with rare honesty the fatigue, the messiness, the slowing down and quiet retreat that is part of menstruation for many. In doing so, she uses these tools of representation to create an alternative visual language for periods within mainstream visual culture. Kaur disrupts the harmful idea that these experiences are shameful or 'disgusting' without glamourising what can be a pretty draining five to seven days. The irony is that – like Collins' and Nicholas-Williams' respective images – in keeping within Instagram's terms of service, Kaur's period-stained sweatpants are not violent, are not nudity and are not an incitement to hate. Yet in publishing these photos, Kaur knew she would attract the ire of those who prefer objectified, non-threatening feminine archetypes to the messy truth of real thing. And she was right.

First came the trolls. Misogyny on full blast, one charmer wrote, 'Come over here and let me make your vagina bleed'.[48] Next, Instagram removed the image not once, but twice. Undeterred, Kaur kept reposting it, thanking the company for 'providing me with the exact response my work was created to critique'.[49] She continued:

> I will not apologize for not feeding the ego and pride of misogynist society that will have my body in an underwear but not be okay with a small leak when your pages are filled with countless photos/accounts where women (so many who are underage) are objectified, pornified and treated less than human.

The outcry generated by Instagram's removal of Kaur's image, exacerbated by their initial refusal to explain their actions, proved impossible for the company to ignore. Kaur's response to the original deletion of her image garnered 53,000 likes and over 12,000 shares.[50] After restoring the image, Instagram wrote to Kaur, saying the image had been removed by a team member in error and apologising for the mistake. What Instagram classed as an 'error' can also be regarded as the result of Kaur testing – and revealing – the limits of what the site considers to be an acceptable feminine body and what it does not.[51]

Kaur's use of Instagram to document a side of women's lives rarely represented (beyond the aforementioned suspicious blue liquid in ads for sanitary products) drew on the radical history of feminist body art. In tone and style, her images are especially evocative of a 1972 installation by Judy Chicago, one of the major feminist artists of the seventies, which you can now see online.[52] Entitled *Womanhouse, Menstruation Bathroom* (part of *Womanhouse*, an installation and performance space Chicago co-organised) it depicts a tidy, spotlessly clean, white-tiled bathroom with sanitary products stacked on its shelves. This orderliness is upset by the presence of a bin to the centre left of the image, stuffed to overflowing with blood-stained pads and tampons, one of which has fallen out and lies on the floor. Of the installation, Chicago said, 'Under a shelf full of all the paraphernalia with which this culture "cleans up" menstruation was a garbage can filled with the unmistakable marks of our animality. One could not walk into the room, but rather, one peered in through a thin veil of gauze, which made the room a sanctum.'[53]

A little over forty years later Kaur used Instagram as a creative tool and virtual space in which to stimulate a similar effect, inviting the viewer to witness experiences women are expected to keep out of sight, hidden away in the domestic sphere. She was far from alone in this. Women have used Instagram to document childbirth, mastectomy scars and breast-feeding, and they too have had their images removed and faced with threats of account closure. Like periods, these experiences are entirely natural yet rarely depicted in the mainstream: when they are, they often trigger responses that treat them as aberrant. To understand why, it is important to emphasise again that technology such as social media is not separate from culture or society – it arises from them, reflecting their preoccupations while shaping those preoccupations in turn.

Unruly women and their unruly bodies have always been viewed as a threat to the established order, where, as journalist Joan Smith writes, 'we teach men that women are inferior from the cradle, and they spend their lives struggling, against the evidence, to convince themselves that this is the case'.[54] Women who defy bodily standards like 'purity', youth, heterosexuality, femininity, thinness – the list goes on – yet demand visibility are especially worrisome, as symbolised in the figure of the 'feminine grotesque'. A storytelling staple in many cultures, the feminine grotesque takes various forms from the witch to the evil stepmother to the old hag to vengeful queens and desirable but deadly women such as the *femme fatale*: she also serves as a gendered lens through which non-conforming femininity is judged to this day. The feminine grotesque stems from a distrust of women's bodies and the feminine world, entities considered 'monstrous' and 'grotesque' because they are 'other' – in other words, not male. Thus, menstrual blood is construed as shameful and unspeakable rather than powerful, which it surely is, symbolising life, death and fertility, processes that reach into every part of human experience. By rejecting this shame, Kaur's images captured the tension the philosopher Julia Kristeva explored in her work on bodies and what she calls 'the abject', where feelings of disgust are not necessarily driven by concerns with cleanliness but with threats to the social order.[55] As Kaur pointed out, her images violated none of Instagram's rules. Instead, they helped illuminate what is assumed but not necessarily articulated by Instagram and the wider culture until provoked – that there are select, predetermined, commercially appealing ways in which the feminine body should be seen, ways that are sexualised, inviting, never threatening. Menstruating is not one of them.

In the last chapter I mentioned the work of comedian Celeste Barber in relation to studies[56] which found that viewing imagery parodying and rejecting the beauty aesthetics of selfie culture can help women mitigate feelings of body shame and self-objectification. But with almost 7.5 million

Instagram followers and global recognition for her work, not even Barber can escape the digital scythe that is Instagram's algorithm. Barber's approach to parody is simple but effective: she recreates impossibly perfect images of celebrities and models, juxtaposing her unadorned ordinariness with their heavily edited, ridiculously posed shots. The results are funny but effective, skewering just how far-fetched and unnatural such imagery is, and emphasising what a great antidote good old reality is to the unreality of Instagram culture. Unfortunately, while her millions of followers get the joke, Instagram's algorithm apparently does not.

In October 2020 Barber posted a shot on the site of her mimicking the pose of a skinny, blonde, half-naked Victoria's Secrets model, in profile, with a hand covering her breast.[57] Unlike the model, Barber wore string bikini bottoms, making her 'less' naked – not that it mattered. In terms of what they revealed – stomach, side-boob but no nipple (phew), some upper thigh – the images were practically identical, but while Barber's shot was censored, the model's image was not. Barber's fans were not allowed to share her post. Instead, some of them received a message telling them that the shot contravened the site's rules on nudity or sexual activity.[58] Clearly, Barber's humour was lost on the algorithm but so too was the wider point she was making about what kinds of visibility Instagram supports. Ironically, the site's treatment of her image made those double standards clear as a blue sky. Writer and plus-sized activist Lacey-Jade Christie, writing about the Barber affair, put it succinctly: 'The Instagram algorithm favours thin, white, cisgender people and effectively censors the rest of us.'[59]

Every day, millions of women take and upload their images to Instagram, most of them hoping for some sort of recognition. They give their time, their effort and their attention to the platform but what they get in return is governed by cultural and technological forces, over which they have little control. But when they study the site they will observe, correctly, that certain types of images are granted greater visibility than others. Desiring that visibility, they may begin to self-edit to produce images that conform to the norm but feel less and less like a fair representation of themselves, creating the kind of fragmentation between self and image that Essena O'Neill described.[60] It's not surprising, then, that research has found Instagram selfies exhibit higher levels of gender-stereotypical behaviour than magazine advertisements[61] and that greater Instagram use is associated with higher levels of self-objectification.[62] Chasing likes in this context can create a reinforcing effect, where users undertake limiting, inauthentic displays of femininity in the hope of achieving a high degree of visibility. It is also exclusionary for those who do not fit neatly into the gender binary or whose identities defy stereotypes. As body-positivity activist Kayla Logan of the Don't Delete My Body! campaign writes on her blog, 'Instagram's biased censorship erases marginalized and progressive people from posting and a lot of times from even having a profile ... who or what are we trying to protect by eliminating marginalized people and progressives from view?'[63]

Given the size of their platforms, their online profiles and their refusal to be silenced, Collins, Nicholas-Williams and Kaur managed to draw lots of much-needed attention to the censorship they experienced. The outcry in Nicholas-Williams' case was so effective that, combined with her activism and international media coverage, it forced Facebook/Instagram to update its policy on nudity to address discrimination against black women and plus-sized bodies.[64] For the average Instagram user, however, generating this kind of response would be difficult if not impossible without a significant follower base and wide attention. Like all social media, following the logic of the market, Instagram rewards popularity with visibility. Those with the most likes and followers garner a level of clout unavailable to the average user. When those with followers in the tens of thousands complain, there is a much higher chance that people will sit up and act, including Instagram itself. When the platform's censorship axe falls on those with smaller followings, finding a critical mass of supporters who are willing to rally on their behalf can be a struggle. Without this, ordinary users are at the mercy of algorithms and moderators which, as seen throughout this chapter, are inclined to reproduce harmful norms while ignoring nuance.

In 2015 American writer and musician Jennifer Williams was interviewed by *VICE* about the Instagram account she was running, titled @menstrual.blood, where users could submit period imagery.[65] Williams told the reporter, 'I first got the idea after seeing the Instagram account @skin.is.in, which is no longer active, but they shared submissions of all kinds of bodies. I just loved seeing people celebrate and photograph parts of their bodies that are usually shamed: hair, stretch marks, scratches, scars, bruises.' Asked if the nature of the account represented a form of 'TMI' or 'oversharing', Williams acknowledged that its approach might not be for everyone but emphasised the need for greater awareness and acceptance of periods. 'The @menstrual.blood account is intentional sharing,' she said. 'I saw Instagram as a good venue to intentionally reach a lot of people and to open up conversation, especially for people who might not have other ways to learn or be exposed.'[66]

When I went looking for @menstrual.blood in the summer of 2020 I couldn't find it so I dropped Williams an email, asking what happened. She told me that in late 2016 or early 2017 (she couldn't remember the exact date) Instagram took the account down on the grounds of 'obscene content', an experience she described over email as 'very frustrating'. Williams pointed out that the account was private, 'so anyone following knew what they were in for and of course I don't find the images obscene but Instagram gets to decide I guess (yet much more obscene content, in my opinion, often gets to stay up)'. Williams, along with friends and followers, did try to appeal the ban, but it felt as if no one was listening: 'Filling out their little form feels like yelling into the void.' When I asked if having a larger public platform might have made a difference in challenging the ban, she wrote back, 'I remember wondering at the time if I should push and keep spreading the word and see if more pressure and more voices would make a difference, but also it felt futile.' Running the account 'took a lot of time and energy', she says. Near the end, Williams had to get friends to help with moderating 'because there were so many submissions and so many trolls'. 'It was magical and fun and powerful while it lasted, though,' she wrote, 'and I lit up whenever I saw people connecting and discussing their bodies in empowered and compassionate and honest ways in the comment section.'

In just a decade Instagram has become part of everyday life for a billion-plus people across the world. Its aesthetics are no longer confined to the internet: they spill into real life, where things that once went largely unphotographed just a generation ago – our food, homes, nights out, daily clothing choices, even our bodies – have become endlessly documentable, shareable, visible as never before. Instagram serves us a feast of images so dazzling and so compelling to our desire to see and be seen that it is easy to forget just how powerfully it governs this new visibility. Content created by women and for women is a huge part of the platform's appeal, but this visibility is channelled through a system that tends to favour fantasy bodies over real ones. This trend existed long before social media, but these platforms are reworking and intensifying these double standards for the digital age. This creates an inevitable tension between many women's desire to use these tools to create new kinds of representations and a formidable visual tradition that economically and culturally values certain bodies while banishing others.

In September 2020, in response to how political and cultural upheaval is changing the way people use the platform, Instagram announced the establishment of a new Equity Team 'focused on algorithmic fairness and equitable product experiences'.[67] A statement from the company's head, Adam Mosseri, said the team will work on developing 'better understanding and addressing bias in our product development' and produce 'new features that respond to the needs of underserved communities'.[68] In response to what the statement called 'perceived censorship[69] on Instagram', Mosseri pointed to 'recently published guidelines'[70] on how it determines the visibility of content on the platform. He added: 'Our hope is that people will better understand why some types of content aren't included in recommendations across Instagram and Facebook, and therefore may not be distributed as widely. We consulted over 50 leading experts specializing in recommendation systems, social computing, freedom of expression, safety, civil and digital rights in developing these guidelines.'[71]

Moderating a platform of Instagram's scale – one that spans a huge, diverse global usership – is not easy. In trying to be all things to all users, Instagram is setting itself a difficult if not impossible task; one it would not be faced with to the same degree if, for example, it were a group of platforms of various sizes catering to specific niches. Like all social media, it is quick to sell self-expression, community and creativity. But when self-expression (inevitably) comes up against cultural and commercial orthodoxies, what wins visibility is that which is already regarded as 'normal' and, above all, popular. In this environment conformity is rewarded, not change – a process that sends a wider, often exclusionary message about what is worthy of visibility and what isn't. Yet the platform's huge success shows that there are many people from an array of underrepresented communities who are hungry for new ways of seeing and being seen. This presents a challenge but also an opportunity to break with old rules governing visual culture by using digital technology to create something more exciting and more representative.

On its 'About' page, Instagram says 'All Are Welcome.'[72] It's a nice sentiment but isn't always the case. When it comes to the visibility Instagram has the power to grant or deny, some are more welcome than others.

Four

Influence

In March 2019 *Forbes* caused a furore when it named 21-year-old Kylie Jenner the youngest ever 'selfie-made' billionaire.[1] 'Selfie-made' was a humorous if predictable play on Jenner's association with the selfie. What rankled commentators was how *Forbes*' wording evoked the idea that Jenner's huge success was solely down to her efforts as a 'self-made' businesswoman. Many were quick to point out Jenner's privileged position as the baby of the Kardashian-Jenner clan, a family who have come to symbolise the American dream in the internet age as no other. Critics argued that to ignore the role of Jenner's high-profile relatives in her ascent to global beauty mogul was to fundamentally misrepresent how she achieved her success. Author Roxane Gay tweeted of the affair, 'It is not shade to point out that Kylie Jenner isn't self-made. She grew up in a wealthy, famous family. Her success is commendable, but it comes by virtue of her privilege.'[2] Sidestepping this sticky issue, Jenner attributed her good fortune to an alternative factor: technology. 'It's the power of social media,' she told *Forbes* in July 2018 in an interview about her dollar-spinning beauty empire. 'I had such a strong reach before I was able to start anything.'[3,4]

Only a fool would discount the role of Jenner's family in her success but her remarks about social media are astute. She and her elder sisters, especially Kim, have shown a prophetic ability to exploit the visibility offered by social media for professional success. In the process the Kardashians have become ambassadors for the hyperfeminine, access-all-areas ethos that has come to define a great deal of what we call 'influencer culture', especially its uppermost echelons. While never describing themselves as feminists, they have instead instrumentalised the movement's spirit, eschewing its politics while building empires premised on wishy-washy notions of female empowerment. Of her million-dollar jeans line for example (which she describes as 'revolutionary') Khloé Kardashian says, 'The line is all about empowerment ... making the women feel great about themselves and embracing women of all shapes.'[5] From a business perspective it's a savvy move, using a fast-changing media landscape to 'sell' visibility as a rewarding lifestyle choice, while also selling solutions to appearance pressures women have long struggled with, which have become heightened under the spotlight of the social media age. The Kardashians – like the vast ecosystem of other high-profile beauty, fashion and lifestyle influencers who emulate them – are on hand to help lesser mortals deal with the demands of the exposure they are so enthusiastic about embracing (and from which they happily profit). This has helped create a lucrative global market, with the influencer industry projected to be valued at $15 billion by 2022.[6]

While 'influencing' can involve any number of fields and skill sets, in mainstream understanding it is most often associated with aspirational images and positivity, 'inspiration' of various sorts that tends to revolve around consumption and the belief that self-branding is what smart twenty-first-century women do. This produces assumptions about 'influencers' that are often unfair and inaccurate. While 'ultra-influencers' like the Kardashians are the most visible proponents of the industry, most influencers do not have anywhere near their clout, resources or earning power. For these creators (many of whom are women), carving out a career in this still-new industry is less about glamour and more about working hard in a highly changeable environment without the supports offered by traditional forms of employment. This has left many influencers and digital creators vulnerable to unscrupulous clients and burnout from unrelenting demand for content, leading to the foundation of the first UK's content creators' trade union in June 2020.[7] Unlike Kylie Jenner, these creators are not billionaires, nor do they have a famous family to fall back on. The UK Bloggers Survey 2019 found that just 18 per cent of influencers were able to live off content creation and their social media presence alone,[8] with another survey showing influencers need a following of at least 42,575 to earn the average industrial wage in the UK of £29,000.[9]

The influencer arrived on the cultural scene at a tumultuous time, shortly after the 2008 financial collapse and just as social media turned the formerly private public. As economic uncertainty intensified, 'going freelance' was touted as a novel way of making a living in a world of spiralling redundancies and seas of unpaid internships, especially for millennials. In this climate, it is no surprise then that the industry trades on a growing yearning for stability, prosperity and of course visibility, through economic and personal success, embodied by the figure of an always-on breed of female entrepreneur slash creative and her picture-perfect life. Unlike other forms of advertising that are explicit in their desire to sell you a product or a lifestyle, the appeal of influencers comes from offering models for living and working that seem more accessible than other forms of celebrity and don't feel as grubby as a 'hard sell', even when the reality is anything but. Many of these individuals market themselves as almost-but-not-quite-ordinary women, or if they are celebrities, they are celebrities whose problems seem relatable and whose lives appear to be an open book.

This iconography, which has shown itself to be highly appealing across the media but especially online, taps into a sentiment that literary scholar Lauren Berlant calls 'cruel optimism': optimism becomes cruel when we are encouraged to invest emotionally and psychologically in objects or ideas that sell a vision or fantasy they cannot deliver.[10] The dream of a middle-class lifestyle, for example, is moving increasingly further out of reach for millennials and the younger generations, thanks to a series of worldwide recessions, a global pandemic and an ailing economic system. Yet across the media this vision of 'the good life' is still being held up as an achievable common goal, ignoring those newly excluded and those who always have been.

Although sold as attainable through hard work, consumerism and fortitude, the truth is that the desirable lifestyles showcased by influencer cultures such as those of Planet Kardashian remain out of the reach of most women. Inevitable disappointments arise from investing in these images of personal and professional success, disappointments for which the only remedy presented is to reinvest in the system by working harder, taking better pictures, changing one's appearance, rethinking your personal brand. Because while social media may seem to have democratised entry to the marketplace and especially the creative industries, in reality these platforms represent a wider economic shift that has seen precarious employment rise starkly while wages and opportunities diminish. This has had an impact on all sections of the economy but particularly fields such as the arts and journalism, the very industries into which social media is presented as the golden ticket. It is no surprise that those most likely to succeed as influencers are those with existing financial and cultural capital to draw on; those who already have an established profile and those who can afford to spend time artfully branding themselves to achieve money-spinning forms of visibility because they don't have to worry about paying rent or keeping the lights on. This presents a situation where conformity and optimism, gussied up as 'empowerment' and 'aspiration', are pushed as the solution to problems they have little actual hope of solving, all while lining the coffers of the already fortunate.

It is not hyperbolic to say that the Kardashians have become a cultural phenomenon, transcending the family itself and the individuals within it to encompass a look and ethos that circulates as much offline as it does online. At its core the family's success reflects major shifts in the media landscape at the turn of the century, beginning with reality television in the 1990s and accelerating with social media from the mid-2000s onwards, where the proliferation of channels and platforms saw the demand for new forms of celebrity and content rise steeply. This change coincided with the arrival onto the cultural scene of Spice Girl 'girl power' and the emergence of an individualistic, choice-focused popular feminism, which still thrives on social media. Where earlier forms of feminism questioned the physical and emotional strictures of femininity, like the expectation women be polished, pleasant and preened in ways men are rarely expected to be, this feminism embraced them on the grounds of 'choice'.

These factors laid the groundwork for what I refer to here as the KIC: the Kardashian Industrial Complex. An industrial complex develops when a business becomes embedded in political institutions or social movements, often in the hope that it will help them achieve their aims. While these institutions or movements are generally dedicated to the betterment of society (by tackling poverty, for example, or improving prison conditions), the business – being a business – is dedicated to the betterment of itself and its shareholders through profit. This creates a tension: the fewer problems political institutions and social movements solve, the more profit there is for businesses who work in this way. This produces a conflict of interest where the business benefits from goals not being reached and problems going unsolved; in fact, it is in the business's interest that it remain this way. The KIC performs in a similar fashion, celebrating and selling visibility as something all shrewd women do, offering a blueprint for how to manage the rising demands for visibility in the digital age that omits any questioning as to why women are being subjected to ever-increasing levels of scrutiny in the first place. The unspoken expectation is that one should *want* to meet this gaze, to revel in it, and should be willing to spend whatever it takes – financially, emotionally, physically – to at least *look* as if you are living your best life as a step towards manifesting it. Empowerment is promised but never fully achieved because if it ever were, there would be little need for the shapewear, detox teas and the lip kits that have made the Kardashians millionaires many, many times over.

It is important to stress here that the KIC is not representative of all social media content created by and for women. Far, far from it. Nor is it representative of all influencers or indeed other types of creators who find themselves lumped under the influencer umbrella. Again, far from it. But it is a ubiquitous, compelling and lucrative form of social media self-branding that trickles down from influencers with the greatest visibility to those with the lowest. In the KIC, notions of privacy are turned on their heads. Self-branding through extreme self-exposure is celebrated, with any dissent – especially any questioning of one's choices – treated with the suspicion that it is anti-woman and therefore must be rooted out. This makes holding the KIC to account a difficult endeavour.

From birth to marriage to children, from gynaecological appointments to familial histrionics to sex to the home, formerly out-of-sight experiences are rendered broadcastable, shareable, commodifiable, supremely *visible* – so long as they prescribe to hyper-glam aesthetics, where 'realness' is represented by millionaires and billionaires who live in mansions and resemble supermodels. The great Nora Ephron once remarked that, for writers, everything in life is copy.[11] For the KIC, everything in life has the potential to be transformed into the content that builds a self-brand. This reflects its origins in reality television where the Kardashians made their first splash – a format that is social media's precursor in many respects, reflecting a point in time when a new kind of celebrity emerged, one created by the media and reliant on the media for its existence. Where older forms of fame were visited on those with exceptional talents or experiences, modern-day celebrity relies heavily on the self as its unique selling point. For the KIC, the process of transforming one's self into a commodity is an essential attention-getting manoeuvre within an economy where attention is all.

What makes the KIC compelling, like so much of women's media, is how it acts as an exemplar for femininity in a world where women are constantly being told they are doing everything wrong. For all its issues, at a time of great uncertainty the KIC offers a captivating script for what society values as 'feminine' in the twenty-first century. But despite its 'empowered' window-dressing, it is a script as problematic as its predecessors. The KIC may be feminine in terms of leadership and audience but it flogs an archetype of an expensive, hypersexualised beauty that is custom-built for a male gaze. It also enshrines the expectation that women alter themselves in ever more intimate ways, normalising invasive procedures such as Botox and lip fillers as just another part of one's beauty regime. This produces a new standard of beauty that is generated by technology and embodied through surgical intervention and intensive grooming. Writer Jia Tolentino calls it 'Instagram face',[12] where the adherence to new forms of beauty uniformity produces an effect that is 'cyborgian'. She writes, 'The face is distinctly white but ambiguously ethnic – it suggests a *National Geographic* composite illustrating how Americans will look like in 2050, if every American were to be a direct descendant of Kim Kardashian, Bella Hadid, Emily Ratajkowski and Kendall Jenner.'[13]

Although it is everywhere in the culture, Tolentino argues that Instagram face is largely only accessible to 'white women capable of manufacturing a look of rootless exoticism'.[14] This manufacturing doesn't come cheap, leading poorer women to risk their health letting unqualified therapists and quack doctors inject them with substances that are dangerous, even lethal if used incorrectly. It also smacks of privilege, where wealthy women can play with marginalised identity codes without ever having to live the reality of them.

Although very much of the moment, the KIC is the latest example of what Simone de Beauvoir once described as the 'eternal feminine':[15] a culturally prescribed notion of female perfection or 'essence' that sits on women's shoulders like a tiny devil, reminding them of all the ways they fail to live up to what society considers to be the ideal. She is both aspirational in that women are told they should desire to be her and self-defeating because no human can match a fantasy that is designed to confound them. The eternal feminine does not die and she certainly does not age. Instead she evolves, letting the gender politics of the era depict her appeal. Where once she espoused the joys of 'having it all' from the pages of Sunday-paper lifestyle supplements, now she espouses the joys of 'showing yourself having it all' from our smartphone screens.

A huge part of what makes the KIC so powerful is how it uses the intimacy and immediacy of social media to connect with a global female audience. On social media, celebrities and even strangers feel accessible to us in ways unimaginable offline. We can see into their homes, their lives, even their souls – even when we know this content is no less produced and strategic than what we see in magazines. This sense of accessibility and connection is central to the KIC's emotional appeal, which relies heavily on the bonds of female relationships. Cultural commentators are often snide rather than analytic in their account of the Kardashians' rise to prominence, ignoring how keenly they understood their audience and the economic potential of social media platforms before the wider commercial world took notice. Kim and co. took formats that many look down on – reality television, social media – and blended them with a feminised brand of entrepreneurialism to build a twenty-first-century empire based on female consumerism. Using the appeal of sisterhood[16] both in terms of their familial ties and their connection to their fans, they reimagined femininity, not as something you do for men but as something you invest in, take control of and put on display for yourself, your friends and your career. They took L'Oréal's 'Because you're worth it' catchphrase and pushed it further, turning femininity into a personal business plan.[17] This aspect of their origins story in particular holds major appeal for women trying to make their way in an increasingly precarious and competitive economic climate, where being your own business makes more and more sense because long-term job security is going the way of the dinosaurs. The problem is that the feminine visibility the KIC sells completely ignores the cultural and economic reasons that make women responsive to its myths. It is a poster child for the excesses of late-stage capitalism and age-old beauty pressure, excesses that place it in another galaxy compared to the realities of most women's lives.

One of the great debates that have raged ever since the KIC came to public prominence is whether it is empowering. The question itself highlights how 'empowerment' has become a lightning rod for the way popular feminism draws inspiration from more rebellious forms but shies away from fully embodying its disruptive potential, watering it down into something far more palatable and sellable like a special-edition lipstick or a pair of shoes that cost more than the minimum monthly wage. This kind of empowerment revolves around the individual's desires (often remedied through consumerism and 'feeling good') as opposed to societal transformation through collective action. Similar to other totems of popular feminism over the last ten years (see Sheryl Sandberg's bestseller *Lean In*[18] and the short-lived reign of the GirlBoss)[19], the KIC urges women to change themselves rather than their world.

While this message is not without merit – taking responsibility for oneself and building a life of purpose, independence and meaning are certainly worthy endeavours – it ignores to the point of hypocrisy how limited this approach can be, especially for women on the margins. It celebrates 'choice' without stopping to consider the underlying forces that enable and constrain women's choices, something that is a daily reality for all but an elite band of women like the sisters Kardashian. Most of us cannot simply 'choose' our way out of a buckling financial system, a lack of affordable, flexible childcare, the failings in women's health services, or inequalities whose roots run centuries deep. With blithe indifference to this fact, the KIC and its ilk sells a version of womanhood where the greatest obstacle to female advancement is the woman herself – which they are on hand to help with. Just circle whatever the issue is – confidence/body shame/self-esteem – and buy whatever it is they're selling to remedy it.

In the main, what the KIC peddles is a vision that is loudly, unapologetically upper-middle class to upper class, where ready access to financial resources buys you the means to create the kind of commercially appealing feminine visibility that thrives on sites such as Instagram. This is, of course, not new. From the art world to advertising to Hollywood, these types of images have always generated huge revenue, and social media is no different. In March 2020 for example, American website *The Intercept* reported that TikTok had been suppressing posts by those it deemed to be too 'ugly' and 'poor' to attract new users to ensure the site's continued growth.[20] On platforms that claim to support creative self-expression (and are certainly happy to profit from it) anyone can join, but not everyone gets to be seen.

Taking 'good' selfies in beautiful locations, developing the skills of personal branding, networking successfully online and offline – these all require the kinds of time, investment, and cultural capital that are beyond the reach of many women who simply cannot afford to play the KIC game. Instead of addressing this complex reality as any form of meaningful feminism or 'empowering' movement should, the KIC instead advocates individualised approaches to structural issues that are heavy on tinkering and light on transforming. Want to change your life? Think positive! Unhappy with your body? Buy shapewear! Worried about your career? Lip fillers will give you confidence! And while you're at it, why not spend fifty bucks on a networking breakfast? For an ethos that is so eager to celebrate visibility, the KIC is far less inclined to acknowledge those it treats as invisible, namely the many women who cannot access or embody its pricey, exclusive brand of femininity. Nor is it particularly kind, despite its sisterly appearance.

Just as women use social media to represent themselves, they also use it to build networks and foster relationships with each other, producing digital public spaces that are markedly more feminised than other forms of media. In these environments the KIC thrives by appealing to notions of sisterhood while projecting what academic Alison Winch calls 'the girlfriend gaze'.[21] This gaze takes the bonds of female friendship (which Western popular culture from the Spice Girls to *Sex and the City* to the *Girls Trip* movie treats as a critical aspect of a woman's identity) and the pleasures of looking at other women and toxifies them, producing what Winch calls a 'gynaeopticon', where girlfriends closely watch how each other performs femininity, bonding over judging and being judged.

As a social-media-based phenomenon, flooded with enticements to watch and critique, the KIC amps up these effects tenfold, channelling pleasurable-looking into judgemental-looking, something it presents as part and parcel of 'doing' femininity. This produces a female gaze that is powerful but not progressive. It may displace the male gaze in these online spaces, but in doing so it produces effects that are no less objectifying or disciplining; for the girlfriend gaze is forensic and brutal in its assessment of how well (or not) a woman is performing her femininity. One only has to have dipped one's toe into the waters of comments sections or private groups on social media, where screenshots and selfies of the unsuspecting are being eviscerated, to know how nasty this culture can be. Being a star doesn't protect you any more than being an ordinary person does. All women are expected to be adept at representing themselves in the right way, so all are held to the same impossible standards.

The interpersonal nature of this gazing, and the way it relies on competitiveness and feedback loops, make criticising it difficult because participation is taken as complicity. It may have a veneer of sisterliness, but the girlfriend gaze is about judgement rather than encouragement. Where feminism emphasises the power of the group, the girlfriend gaze makes solidarity difficult by casting women as spectacles to be surveyed and critiqued by each other rather than men – an endless competition in which all are inevitably found wanting. It is not surprising that Winch describes the girlfriend gaze as the male gaze's handmaiden.[22]

Essena O'Neill was one of the first influencers to issue what Jia Tolentino calls the 'anti-Instagram statement',[23] a now-common occurrence where an individual with a large following and a high-profile announces, with a good dash of drama, their departure from social media. The reason most often offered to their followers is that, as Tolentino writes, Instagram has become 'a bottomless pit of personal insecurity and anxiety'. But this resolve to leave is often less than absolute: 'She'll take a week-long break from the social network, and then, almost always, she will go on exactly as before. Resistance to a system is presented on the terms of the system.'[24]

The internet is awash with these sorts of statements. During my research I came across variations of it from women who described themselves as 'influencers', 'content creators' or 'bloggers' living all over the world. Most often, these women where not the high-profile influencers Tolentino writes about. They had a lot more to lose by stepping back even for a short while from a platform like Instagram, which has become Ground Zero for influencer and creator cultures of all stripes, from fashion to travel to food. Celebrities bidding adieu to Instagram is one thing: I wanted to know why less high-profile creators were taking this step. I also wanted to know what they thought about so many others appearing to do the same. Is it simply a trend, capitalising on a growing ambivalence towards social media, cannily extracting more engagement from one's followers by rejecting said engagement, if only for a time? Or is it a genuine response to the emotional and time costs of being visible online, something influencers and content creators know a lot more about than most?

'I realised I needed to take a break from Instagram when it began to feel like an obligation that I dreaded rather than something I truly enjoyed.'

Christina is a travel blogger who announced her intention to quit Instagram on her blog in 2018. As her websites are the main source of her income, she could afford to take a step back; but it wasn't simply a matter of finances: 'When I first started out, I saw Instagram as a fun place to share photos on the go and find a community with similar interests. Somewhere along the way though, Instagram went from being "Insta" to an aspirational mood board of increasingly professional, edited and staged photos.' Over email, Christina tells me that these changes on the platform produced 'pressure to conform to these new standards', mentioning the notorious algorithm change in 2016:

> Adding to this pressure, of course, was the introduction of a new mysterious algorithm that dictated what people saw in feeds rather than the purely chronological feed that Instagram started with. This created a 'new normal' where creators were fighting to be seen in this algorithm, yet oftentimes seeing numbers sink lower and lower for no apparent reason. For many, myself included, this really sucked the fun out of the platform.

Over time, Christina felt her labour could be better spent elsewhere:

> I think many creators, like me, have realised what a time drain Instagram can be, and how there are so many ways to generate income beyond Instagram that are much more worth my time. For example, sometimes a single Instagram photo can take hours to capture, edit, caption and post. Even if that post is sponsored, that's a one-off payment that will not bring you any more income in the future. In contrast, if I spend those same hours writing a blog post that ranks well in search engines, that post can potentially bring me ad and affiliate revenue for years to come. Depending on your business, Instagram might not be the best fit, and I think many digital creators are beginning to realise that.

Natalie is a writer and researcher who corresponded with me over email from the United States. In the last few years she felt her relationship with Instagram sour and was moved to write about it. For her, changes to the app (the Stories feature, for example) have made it a burdensome, time-wasting 'sinkhole':

> It's no longer just having photos come up on our feed and deciding whether to like them or not, there's an element where we feel we 'have to' follow certain people and find out what they are doing. I definitely felt that the time I was spending on Instagram could be used more productively, and that 'switching off' in the evenings was important for my relationship with my husband, who doesn't use Instagram.

Reimagining her relationship to Instagram and social media more broadly became about establishing firmer boundaries around what to share but also questioning the need to share in the first place:

> Even if you aren't an 'influencer', I find that there is a great deal of curating that goes on to create content for Instagram. We need to get back to enjoying a cup of coffee, picking an outfit, eating lunch etc. without feeling the need to share it online. Our enjoyment of it isn't diminished simply because we don't share it online! I think more and more people are choosing to step back from social media – and Instagram in particular – because they are becoming more aware of the dangers of using it. Perceived 'dangers' don't have to be well, dangerous, but they can be a growing awareness of the sheer amount of time we spend online; worry about sharing our locations/routines online with strangers; or sharing pictures of children.

For Natalie, these concerns were very present rather than purely philosophical, as she explained:

> I am now expecting a baby and my shift away from Instagram has definitely changed the way I feel about sharing details about my life on the internet more widely. My husband and I have agreed that there are many ways for people we know to feel involved and included in our lives without posting pictures of our baby online. I think lots of people feel this way or are coming to the realisation that sharing every part of their lives is undesirable.

While the KIC presents self-branding through visibility as a positive, turning yourself into a commodity comes with high emotional and time costs, as many influencers (current and former) understand only too well. Verity is a writer, TV presenter and media personality from New Zealand who has written about what it is like to be an influencer, drawing from both her own experiences and those of others. Over email I ask her what prompted her to call time on her experience of the industry. Pulling no punches, she tells me:

> The slowly dawning but utterly inescapable realisation I was living life not as a human but a brand – making decisions in my daily life in order to position it a certain way for Brand Verity, and being so concerned with that day to day that it took over my emphasis on actually living. I couldn't walk past a wall without analysing it for photo opportunities.

Looking back on her time as an influencer, she says, 'I honestly don't think it's sustainable for humans to live as brands; it requires a whole team to sustain and a complete willingness to flatten down and erase the more interesting, complicated and ultimately human parts of your personality.' Then there's the unrelenting, always-on nature of the industry and the absence of time for anything else:

> Personally, I found the pace and scale of content creation you need to sustain influencer life overwhelming. You need a team and your own willingness to iron out and erase your flaws, complications and contradictions – which is ultimately what makes us human, right? Also, you just can't tell the truth

> about how you feel, you always have to filter every statement through your own internal PR team. And lastly, you just don't enjoy your life anymore. Every date, coffee, catch-up, run, book-reading session or phone call with your mum changes from something personal into 'content' and that bleaches the fun out of your life.

I ask Verity to say a little more about something she wrote in one of her articles, that 'the more instafamous you get, the more instafamous you need to be'.[25] She says:

> I think that's probably, one, a reflection that Instafame is designed to be as addictive as possible, with algorithms to keep you engaged and ever-scrolling and the idea that your success as a brand/person is predicated on the constant growth of your follower count and engagement. And that is addictive as it suggests progress is constant growth – and that's measured in 'fame'. Two, Instafame is just a strange, easier-to-achieve version of 'real fame' or 'old-school fame', where you're a celebrity. And the very nature of real fame is that the more you get, the more you need, because at its heart, it's an illusion. And one that moves ever further out of reach the more you grasp for it.

In their responses, Christina, Natalie and Verity highlight something that is often missed when it comes to influencer cultures: the colossal amount of emotional and creative labour that goes into being active in these online spaces, a great deal of which is performed by women. This work is critical to social media's business model but only a lucky few are ever remunerated for it to the extent that they can make a career out of it. Communications researcher Brooke Erin Duffy calls it 'aspirational labor', where female content creators believe 'that their mostly (unpaid) work, motivated by passion and the infectious rhetoric of entrepreneurialism, will eventually yield respectable income and rewarding careers'.[26] While the promise of this sort of labour is an alluring prospect, it is not one is that is easily achieved. As Duffy writes, the term highlights the gap between 'this belief and the practical realities of the digital labor marketplace: just a few digital content creators reap significant material reward for their activities'.[27] In this tough environment, would-be influencers and ambitious content-creators are expected to manage not only their image but their emotions, to espouse positivity and resilience at every turn, to truly embody the belief that anyone can make it if they just try hard enough, despite all the evidence to the contrary. There is no room for bad days, bad moods, mistakes, contradictions or the unexpected, the very things that are, as Verity put it, 'ultimately what makes us human, right?' In such a context, refusing visibility might be just another act of self-branding or it could be an entirely legitimate, genuine response to forms of exposure and promises drenched in cruel optimism that would rattle even the most emotionally robust among us. By rejecting this type of visibility, we take back control.

In Tolentino's account, the anti-Instagram statement is generally followed by a return. 'She'll take a week-long break from the social network,' she writes of the leavers, 'and then, almost always, she will go on exactly as before.'[28] Part of this is, of course, social media's agenda-setting grip on contemporary culture. Celebrities rely on it more and more; abandoning it outright is never going to be an option for them unless they transcend to superstardom. For many influencers, it is literally their bread and butter.

But could it also be that a return sometimes marks a shift towards making Instagram and other social media work on your terms, rather than the other way around? For example, Christina still uses her Instagram, but very differently than she used to:

> I think the main change is that I no longer feel the pressure to post something perfect every single day. This was one of the main reasons I burned out and had to take a break. Instead, I'm purposeful with my usage of the platform. I think of my goal first, whether it's to promote a new article, or even just for fun, and then I build around that. Senseless posting on Instagram is no longer part of my business strategy, and it honestly is such a freeing feeling!

Natalie has also kept her Instagram, not for the visibility it offers but for keeping in contact with friends and family:

> My use of Instagram now is actually as a messaging service. I much prefer it to Facebook messenger, as it is much easier to carry a conversation and react to other people's responses. As a Brit living in the US, I can find it difficult to maintain friendships and stay in touch with friends who are far away and in a different time zone. I'm glad the potential for direct/private conversations exists through Instagram, and if it didn't, I'd probably delete the app altogether!

When I ask Verity if she will ever return to influencing, she replies: 'I rarely use social media now, and when I do it's always for work, as in, "Here's a link to an exhibition I just put on." Reframing it as a professional tool, not a personal branding exercise, helped me reclaim my sanity and stops me falling into this bottomless pit of narcissism and self-disgust that living as a personal brand often entails.'

Searching the #fitspo and #fitspiration hashtags on Instagram in the early autumn of 2020 yields over 71 million hits and over 18 million hits respectively. It also produces a sense of personal slovenliness. Thanks to working from home during the pandemic, I've become an athleisure slob, living in exercise clothing while doing little in the way of actual exercise. Scrolling through the countless images of athleticism the platform offers up, from lean midriffs to chiselled biceps to convoluted yoga poses, I become aware of my horribly crouched posture, stomach flab and lapsed gym attendance. If I were seeking motivation to do something about my lockdown-induced laziness, my Instagram timeline offers no end of inspirational quotes. 'Inhale confidence, exhale doubt,' says the first, implying that confidence is something to be consumed while doubt is something to cast out rather than listen to. 'The distance between your dreams and reality is called action,' proclaims the next. 'Live your dream,' urges another, with no instruction on how someone stuck in a tiny flat in the middle of a global pandemic with a dwindling bank balance might endeavour to do so. 'Your health is an investment, not an expense,' bellows yet another, showing an image of a woman balancing on her head, her upside-down smile a picture of serenity.

A feminine archetype is emerging in these image quotes. Photogenic, driven, positive to a fault, an advocate of hard work and impenetrable self-belief, she trains her body as fiercely as she trains her mind. She takes 'my body is a temple' to a whole other level, subscribing to restrictive diets, superfoods and supplements she believes will keep her in peak physical condition, a journey she shares with followers who are keen to do the same. Everything in her life, even her snacks and sweaty workout gear, look like the pages of an expensive lifestyle catalogue. Her displays are just as ostentatious as Lady Bountiful, so I christen her Lady Wellness, the most visible proponent of an influencer culture that orientates around nutrition, fitness and 'well-being', part of an industry that is now worth $4.5 trillion.[29]

In the 2019 edition of her book *Bodies*, the psychotherapist and author Susie Orbach writes, 'Our bodies have become a form of work. *The body is turning from being the means of production to the production itself* [emphasis Orbach's].'[30] As Orbach captures, where our bodies were once the means through which we experienced the world, they are increasingly a project in themselves requiring the endless 'investment' of our time, labour, financial resources and emotions. Bodily discipline is not new, especially for women, but what is new is the heightened scrutiny bodies and appearances undergo in an era when smartphones allow the individual to watch themselves and others as never before, enabling us to carve up the body for forensic levels of on-screen dissection. The KIC sees this development as a positive – all part of investing in yourself, sister – comparing working on one's body to working on one's career. It's just another part of a woman's self-brand. Lady Wellness is also indicative of this perspective, repackaging dieting and self-objectification as a type of self-care, as something a woman chooses to do *for herself* as part of a successful life. Like its predecessors, today's thriving online diet and exercise culture presents itself as a supportive, inspiring, if rather show-offy friend ready to help you master your 'defective' body. As Orbach writes: 'For ordinary women – and it's more usually women – who are dysmorphic and distressed, online forums have replaced reality-TV shows in providing an opportunity to compete over body distress and win the prize of radical restructuring from head to toe.'[31]

This type of 'self-care' is generally not the kind promoted by Audre Lorde, an originator of the concept, who emphasised the importance of spiritual nourishment and loving oneself as a political act.[32] The self-care Lorde advocated for are practices that act as ballast in the face of serious illness (she battled cancer), racism, sexism and homophobia in a world hostile to difference. By contrast, Lady Wellness shills fancy tracksuits, juices that cost as much as a bag of groceries and exclusive yoga retreats on the Balearic Islands because she sees self-care not simply as a practice to be cultivated but as a series of experiences and 'things' to be purchased on the path to a 'better' self. Where Lorde's concept of self-care, with its roots in counterculture philosophies, contests the dominance of systems like capitalism, Lady Wellness sits firmly within them. Life, as she sees it, is a venture to be optimised at every turn and displayed for others who are similarly invested in the system. Bad thoughts and disruptive feelings are to be mantra-ed and journaled out of existence. Her idea of 'transformation' is squarely focused on the body and the self, not on society. Always faulty even when it is perfectly healthy, the body exists to be laboured over and exposed to judgement; it is a project without end and an expensive one at that. As one of the many, many inspirational quotes in my Instagram feed put it, 'Don't wish for a good body, *work for it*.'

Lady Wellness existed long before social media. From the shiny leotards of Jane Fonda's eighties workout videos to the skeleton worship that was heroin chic in the nineties and size zero in the noughties to Bridget Jones' penchant for counting calories, cigarettes and alcohol units, popular culture's fascination with female bodily discipline is far from new. What is different about social media is how neatly its design supports and reinforces the kinds of extreme behaviours advocated by many diet and exercise enthusiasts, making them visible in new and not particularly healthy ways. Where once Bridget Jones[33] recorded her calorie intake in her diary, now she can share it online, creating a public timeline of her dieting successes and failures. She can add 'before' and 'after' photographs of her unruly body to Instagram or post pictures of her attempts to cook nutritionally balanced, fat-free meals or the number of steps her Fitbit records on any given day. She can observe the weight-loss journeys of others, feeling inspired and despairing in the process. Not only does she count calories and kilos, modern-day Bridget also counts likes, shares and comments. These can be supportive, but sometimes they are downright horrible. On social media, Bridget's 'battle' with her body weight becomes quantified and broadcasted as if it were a news segment she is charged with reporting.

On social media, diets and exercise are public affairs and communal experiences, all watched over by Lady Wellness types, an army of bodily-discipline oracles, all clad in chic workout gear. These women appear to effortlessly inhabit the kinds of bodies that get the most visibility online and elsewhere, symbolising not just physical success but also economic and spiritual success.

That these activities often take place under the guise of having a 'positive body image' makes them tricky to unpack. Justifiable flak has long been levelled at the diet industry, for example, given its obsession with extreme thinness and dubious food fads. Online, however, the distinction between the industry and the individual becomes blurred as the pursuit of a 'positive body image' becomes part of a woman's identity and for wellness influencers, integral to their business model. Given that a large part of the appeal of influencers is their being perceived as more accessible than other types of celebrities, this muddies the waters considerably. Is it an industry that is convincing me to eat kale and give jade eggs a go, or a cheerful-looking, medium-level influencer in a 'Healthy is the New Skinny' T-shirt with affiliate links in her bio and perhaps an #ad hashtag on her image? The former is a vast corporate entity that is well known for preying on people's insecurities and a large part of the reason why having a positive body image can feel transgressive. In a world that tells you to hate yourself, learning not to can be a powerful act. The latter looks super fit but friendly and a lot more human, like she might have my best interests at heart. They couldn't possibly be part of the same thing, could they?

'With Instagram, people almost forget that not everything is there to honestly make them feel good about themselves, even if it looks like people are trying to make them feel good about themselves.' Jacqueline Campion is an eating-distress practitioner and recovery coach. I first interviewed her for a magazine piece on orthorexia back in 2015. Orthorexia is an under-researched dieting condition that has been linked to rising social media use, where healthy eating is taken to extremes. When I put it to her that the current fascination with cultivating a positive body image and achieving 'wellness' has a dark undercurrent, she agrees, pointing out that phenomena including obsessing over food and disordered eating are centuries old. 'The more you talk about food, the more you're focused on food,' she says simply. 'I think there is a blurred line of objectification where we keep the conversation on our bodies.' This leads Jacqueline to ponder, 'Are we meeting objectification with objectification?'

Some forms of objectification work from the outside in. The classic male gaze, for example, is projected onto women to sexualise them and to control them. John Berger thought that women then imbibed this gaze so it worked from the inside out as well as the outside in. But the idea that the male gaze is so totalising as to be the primary way that women 'see' themselves is pretty depressing. After all, although the female gaze has struggled for expression throughout the centuries, from art to literature to photography and beyond, it still managed to assert itself albeit it without the cultural recognition and remuneration granted to its male counterpart. As discussed in the last chapter, women's attempts to use Instagram to project a female gaze that challenges feminine stereotypes has often met with resistance. Against a culture that has awfully specific gender, racial and classed ideas about what women should and should not look like, these images are distinctive in their refusal to cast women's bodies that defy these classifications as flawed or disgusting. In doing so, they reject objectification by asserting their uniqueness – something every human has – to expand the representational field and by extension, what we consider normal. However, as Winch's 'girlfriend gaze' shows, feminine ways of looking are not automatically resistant to the status quo, nor are they necessarily kind. Case in point: how the kinds of visibility promoted by Lady Wellness are channelled through ways of seeing that are forensically critical, regularly misinformed when it comes to nutritional science, and obsessed in the main with the same old slim body ideal.

On a rainy afternoon I chat over Skype with Pixie Turner, aka @pixienutrition on Instagram. Now a nutrition counsellor and trainee therapist who holds a Bachelor of Science in Biochemistry and a Master of Science in Nutrition, for a time in her late teens and early twenties Pixie was a well-known UK wellness influencer who followed a strict plant-based diet. That was until an unsettling encounter with an anti-vaxxer led her to question her beliefs around food, resulting in a professional and personal transformation. 'I was just so stressed,' she says of her time in the wellness industry. 'I was thinking about food so much; food preparation was taking such a long time'. She describes making a beautiful bowl of porridge, only for it to be cold by the time she had finished photographing it: 'It's not a very pleasing existence to be honest, it's just stressful. There was a lot of anxiety around what to eat [and] spending time with people who have the same sorts of insane food rules, the same way I did. We were just exacerbating and reinforcing each other.'

For Pixie, wellness wasn't just about food, it was about finding a community with an outlook that supported her own:

> Social media, especially Instagram, massively reshaped what my idea of normal was. When all of this started, I was nineteen and at uni. There were people around me who were eating in all sorts of different ways but that didn't affect me. That didn't actually influence

> me. I found those people on social media and I took them from online to offline to maintain that consistency. But it was Instagram that had all that power to shape what was normal food wise or what should be normal. Perhaps it was partly aspirational, like this is what normal eating should be, this is what should be normal when it comes to health – why isn't everyone doing this?

Pixie's devotion to wellness began to unravel when she left the UK to travel through India and South East Asia before arriving in Australia where she worked in a vegan health-food shop. Time spent travelling reduced the time she spent on social media and it also put distance between her and the wellness community she had become so involved in at home. It helped to create the mental and geographical space she says was critical to her revaluating her role as a wellness influencer. This accelerated when her friend, a fellow wellness fanatic, turned out to be anti-vaxxer. Coming from a science background this shocked Pixie, leading her to question the perspectives of the community she had invested so much of herself in, a process that saw her faith it in fall apart.

'I started shifting what I was saying on social media really, really slowly, very, very carefully,' she says of her slow pivot out of the wellness industry. 'And at first it worked really well. Stealth mode was fully activated and successful – but then I posted a picture of a fried egg and all hell broke loose.' Cue a slew of unfollows in the thousands and some very upset messages: 'I was a despicable human being. I was disgusting. People were saying I was a fraud. They felt betrayed. It was very, very intense.' The prospect of losing her large following was not something Pixie relished but there was another reason she hoped her followers would stick around during the transition: 'I didn't want to lose those people because I was the one who had contributed misinformation and spread misinformation to them. And I felt if I could retain as many of those people as possible, I could try and undo some of that.'

Calling this time 'a challenge', Pixie nevertheless stuck to proceeding down the path she was tentatively carving out for herself. Doing so prompted a shift in perspective:

> [I realised] actually it's not particularly healthy for me to have such rigid rules and expectations and anxiety around food. Once I started to relax a little bit, I suddenly realised just how much more enjoyable food [and] my life became – so much easier. It was only at that point that I really could see the contrast. I could see that this isn't scientifically accurate, nor is it healthy for me.

It wasn't just posting about the joys of 'forbidden' foods such as cheese, but fighting nutrition misinformation with facts:

> I gradually peppered it throughout – here are some myths about organics, here are some myths about the alkaline diet, that sort of thing. I started putting out these myth-busting posts and started writing about the issues with the wellness industry and also with social media and how there are all these unqualified bloggers giving advice on social media. And I suddenly realised, I'm a bit of a hypocrite, telling people not to listen to all these unqualified

> bloggers and here I am, technically an unqualified blogger.

Enrolling in a Master of Nutrition programme when she returned from Australia meant she 'no longer felt like a hypocrite'. When I ask Pixie if she ever misses the community that was once so much a part of her life, she says 'I found a new community' of activists, doctors, psychologists and nutrition researchers who are as passionate about science communication as she is. Although Instagram played a key role in her immersion in the wellness community, she has not abandoned it. Instead, she uses her platform to tackle misinformation, promote science-based approaches to nutrition and counsel her followers about the interplay between social media, disordered eating and body image.

'I think one of the main reasons why I've been able to continue on Instagram is because it's very clear that I'm no longer an influencer. My role on social media has completely shifted,' she says:

> If I was still an influencer, I wouldn't be comfortable with that, but I'm a healthcare professional first and foremost. As part of that, I feel that I have a certain duty to be a science communicator because I'm good at communicating and because I have the platform. So, whereas at first I was just, you know, an influencer who shared food pictures, now I'm a healthcare professional. My page is no longer an aspirational page, it's a science page. It's completely different. There's this beautiful kind of separation of the two that I think makes it possible for me to feel comfortable and be able to sleep at night, knowing

> I'm on social media and have the influence on the platform that I do.

In May 2020 *Forbes* revoked Kylie Jenner's 'youngest selfie-made billionaire' crown after finding what it said were discrepancies between Jenner's reported wealth and her actual finances.[34] In a statement to the magazine, the Kardashians called *Forbes*' assertions 'absolutely false'.[35] Around the same time I read an article[36] on the BBC website about influencer burnout and the growing numbers of those exiting the industry. Among the reasons cited for this development were the unending demands for content and unpredictable income streams combined with followers' demands for accessibility and authenticity.

When the pandemic hit, I came across another article[37] in the press about the topic by writer and content creator Adele (@adelewalton121 on Twitter). She described how being locked down was contributing to a sense among influencers and content creators (herself included) that they should be creating content all the time along with guilt for not working hard enough. Speaking to Adele over the phone, I asked her how this type of burnout feels. 'I was going in this cycle,' she said, 'I'll have a week of producing content and being really present online. And then suddenly I'd feel really, really low and hopeless.' To counter this, Adele deleted her social media apps off her phone in an effort to try and reconnect with 'the real world'. 'For me [burnout] is a sense of exhaustion, overworking, feeling restless all the time, anxious and low self-worth,' she explained, describing the hamster wheel that is content creation:

> Despite the fact that you're putting out content that is high quality or content that at the time,

> you're happy with, but then feeling that it's never enough. When you're trying to build your platform, it becomes a livelihood for you and your brand or your business is all online, so you feel like you can never stop.

Adele describes the pressure to produce but also the pull of social media, the sense that if you aren't refreshing, scrolling or posting, you are somehow at risk of failing by not being sufficiently online. Then there is the simple fact that, although often dismissed as frivolous because of its feminised nature, influencing – like most roles in the media and creative arts – is hard work, especially if you want to make a living from it. Speaking as a twenty-something who has grown-up consuming influencer culture, Adele says of her generation, 'we see other people doing content creation and we look at ourselves and if you are, you know, naturally outspoken or creative and you enjoy creating content, the possibility of it being something you can make money from becomes quite exciting'. In practice, this means doing not one but a range of roles:

> You are your own PR manager. You are your own everything. I wouldn't say influencing is more difficult than other jobs, but I would say it's so new that it's very much something people are learning to navigate single-handedly. That's why it makes it more difficult to balance the mental health side of things, because there is that blur between work and play. Whereas if you have a nine to five, you know, it's nine to five, these are my hours so when I get home, I can relatively switch off. But if we have our

> phones on us all the time, and if you're a content creator, knowing when to step back and when you're not working, it's kind of impossible.

Chatting to Jacqueline about the problems with wellness culture, she says something that really sticks with me:

> I watch and I think, is this doing the real work? We still keep it at surface level. That's why it's really important to go inward with your posts and your consumption of posts and ask, well, how is this influencing my thoughts, feelings and behaviours? Is it helping, honestly? What is it within us that is driving this? Why are we craving validation from external sources?

It's a similar approach to that taken by Christina, Natalie, Verity and Pixie, who each created space to step back, question and reimagine what their relationship with social media could be, based on figuring out what they – as individuals and professionals – needed from it, rather than letting the platform or the expectations of influencer culture lead the way.

For some influencers and indeed some ordinary folk, the demands of social media visibility eventually become so disorientating and overwhelming that no amount of reframing its place in their lives will suffice. For their actual well-being, they may be inclined to reject it wholesale (if they can afford to), which many do for periods of time, or reduce their presence to lurking rather than sharing or outwardly participating. The pandemic is also reshaping attitudes to the industry as the glamour and indulgence the KIC promotes becomes even more removed from the lives of its followers.

Case in point, the worldwide eyeroll at Kim Kardashian's lavish fortieth birthday celebrations, which took place mid-pandemic and, according to *InStyle*, 'involved a private jet, a private island, and private villas for her and her closest friends and family'.[38] This was followed by widespread backlash in January 2021 towards influencers posting pictures of themselves frolicking on the beach in Dubai while most people were cooped up indoors in the middle of yet another lockdown.[39] At a time of profound economic and personal crisis across the world, 'aspiration' is fast becoming even more of an empty promise. As Izzy Farmiloe, strategy director of Dazed Media, remarked to the *Observer* when discussing the role of influencing in a world besieged by the coronavirus, 'Buying stuff is not what's important right now. It's all about people who stand for something, beyond just trying to promote and push a product.'[40]

In line with all great advertising campaigns, the KIC keeps inconvenient facts and what it considers to be the ugly bits firmly out of shot. It mimics feminism but provides no meaningful substitute, while intensifying the beauty regimes, body shame, objectification and class politics feminism has long critiqued. It dazzles with images of the good life that are out of reach for all but a select few, serving up a dead-end phantasmagoria at a moment when we desperately need new political and economic visions. This disconnect is growing. In September 2020, just as a Kinsey Institute[41] report warned that the pandemic could set gender equality back decades, Kim Kardashian added another product to her empire: maternity shapewear. Writing in the *Irish Times*, Jennifer O'Connell criticised Kim's 'wholehearted endorsement of corsets and concealment, reminders of a Victorian era when women went into "confinement" during their final months [of pregnancy]', observing that, 'These days, you don't need to go into confinement to make your pregnancy publicly acceptable. You can just pick up Kim's €55 "maternity sculpting bodysuit" instead. But why would you bother?'[42] At a time when women's rights are facing their greatest rollback in recent history, it's a question that resonates.

Five

Misogyny 2.0

In August 2014 a host of female celebrities including Jennifer Lawrence, Rihanna and the model Kate Upton became victims of one of the world's most notorious phone-hacking scandals. Christened 'the Fappening' – a portmanteau word of 'happening' and 'fap' (meaning 'to masturbate' in internet parlance) – it saw hundreds of private images stolen from iCloud accounts of high-profile women shared across the internet. Many of these photographs were intimate communications involving nudity, never destined for any audience beyond the women themselves or their partners or former partners. Beginning on the imageboard 4chan, the leak rapidly spread to forums such as Reddit and myriad social media platforms. Despite the questionable legality surrounding how these images were procured and the obvious harm to the women involved, they circulated across mainstream sites with a seemingly unstoppable voyeuristic fervour. Reddit, for example, one of the world's most popular discussion boards, only took the images down due to a deluge of copyright claims.[1] Prior to that, it defended its hosting of them on the grounds of 'free speech', something that enabled the images to be viewed on the site a reported 250 million times before they were removed.[2]

Despite the gross privacy violations on display and the distress of the victims, not everyone was sympathetic to the women involved, especially online. The usual admonishments were trotted out, including attempts to 'slut-shame' those involved as naive narcissists who didn't have the smarts to navigate technology safely (unlike men, naturally) or treat them as celebrities who had no right to be upset since they were already public property, happy to trade on the audience's fascination with them when it suits, whingeing about privacy when it doesn't. The patronising logic was clear. *Why would anyone take a nude picture in the first place? … Why would they then send it to someone? … Come on girls, this is risky behaviour. Something like this was bound to happen eventually – everyone knows that's what you get for being reckless.*

As is so often the case when it comes to discussions of violence against women, these reproaches ignored the motivating force behind the hacks and the conditions that enabled the images to circulate unabated for days: the pathological need some men have to control women, to belittle them, to watch them and ultimately reduce them to sex objects; a culture that is still ill-equipped to deal with their worst excesses; and new forms of technology that enable them to violate the victims' psychological and physical space as never before. As Lena Dunham tweeted in the aftermath of the Fappening, 'The "don't take naked pics if you don't want them online" argument is the "she was wearing a short skirt" of the web.'[3]

Where once the publication of nude images meant an almost certain end to a woman's public career (in 1984 it was why the first African American Miss America, Vanessa Williams, was stripped of her crown) the women caught up in the Fappening were not shamed into silence, nor did they have their careers destroyed. Among the most vocal about what had happened to her was then 24-year-old Jennifer Lawrence, who was at the time the highest-paid actress in Hollywood. According to reports, Lawrence had in the region of fifty images stolen, many of them nudes. In an interview with *Vanity Fair*, she called the hacking and the public's viewing of the images not a scandal but a sex crime, a rationale that made it clear exactly who the guilty parties were. Speaking about the hack impact on her, she said:

> The law needs to be changed, and we need to change. That's why these websites are responsible. Just the fact that somebody can be sexually exploited and violated, and the first thought that crosses somebody's mind is to make a profit from it. It's so beyond me. I just can't imagine being that detached from humanity. I can't imagine being that thoughtless and careless and so empty inside.[4]

A few days after the Fappening, as criminal investigations into the hack swung into action, journalist Amanda Hess wrote about what she observed after a day spent on AnonIB, the imageboard where Lawrence's images first surfaced. What she found was not merely a platform but a thriving community of mainly young men bonded by a desire to violate the privacy not just of celebrities but ordinary women and girls. In an account that makes for grim reading, Hess describes a world of male indifference to female suffering: 'This is a sport, and women are the trophies.'[5] According to Hess, on AnonIB hacking and posting photographs of unsuspecting victims is callously termed a 'win'.[6] Women are not human beings with feelings, lives and reputations; whether acquaintances, college mates or strangers, they are simply targets to be identified and exploited, reduced to images they have no control over; images these men can store and share as they see fit. The dehumanisation is so total that the men Hess observed exhibited little awareness of the harms they were committing. Rather, as she writes, 'they think that they're simply engaging in harmless masturbation; the power differential inherent in their activities is so normalised it probably goes unnoticed'.[7]

Although those suspected of being behind the Fappening have been apprehended, the mess they helped create remains all over the internet. Typing 'the Fappening' into Google in October 2020, one is greeted by any number of sites claiming to have images from the original leak, alongside other questionably procured photographs of famous women. The number-one search result is '#TheFappening: Nude Leaked Celebrity Photos!', boasting an unnerving level of enthusiasm for the stolen material it insists on circulating. Clicking on it reveals a gallery of instantly recognisable women, all naked or close to it. These images are not the thing of photoshoots or red carpets or even private events with friends and family; taken in bedrooms and bathrooms, they are intimate, personal and in some cases quite raw, clearly not intended for public consumption. Yet six years after the Fappening, with perpetrators jailed, these images are still circulating on the vast network that is the internet, viewable by anyone with Wi-Fi access anywhere in the world. These photographs are of some of the wealthiest, best-known women on the planet yet for all their resources, not even they can stop their ongoing distribution. Although stolen and circulated without the consent of their creators, these images appear to be beyond the reach of any legal, ethical or technological mechanism capable of taking them down once and for all.

Just as celebrities find it difficult to fight back against this kind of violation, so too do ordinary women and girls. The surveillance and circulation of images enabled by digital technologies make the male gaze of pre-internet days seem quaint by comparison, back when men who get their kicks from objectifying women largely relied on magazines and videos that had to be purchased and consumed in private. While they could certainly gawp at women, photographing them as they went about their daily lives was difficult and risky, although some certainly tried. Today, in a world where everyone carries not just a camera but a highly sophisticated, discreet, Wi-Fi-enabled camera, any pervert with a smartphone can create objectifying images of a woman without her knowledge or consent. Not only that, he can now distribute them with a single click not just to his friends but across the internet.

Hiding behind the cloak of anonymity, self-described 'creeps' use new technology to create a digital playground of communities such as AnonIB that revolve around predatory gazing. This captures the visibility trap's cruellest contradiction: how the digital tools that put the power of representation in the hands of women as never before can also be used by misogynists to violate and humiliate them in ways unimaginable a generation ago. Misogyny is not merely hating women; it springs from a need to control and maintain a traditional gender order in which women are forever subservient to men. In the West over the twentieth century and into the twenty-first, great strides have been made to cast off the vestiges of patriarchy, but its legacy persists. Although a minority, there are still too many men, and indeed some women, who believe that the female of the species should be seen but never heard, and they have found kindred spirits online. It is a bittersweet irony that new technologies, which have been so useful for feminists and women of all stripes who want to make themselves heard, have reignited an ancient force that exists, as philosopher Kate Manne writes, 'to enforce and police women's subordination and uphold male dominance'.[8]

These communities are not confined to obscure boards on the fringes of the internet. They also operate right under our noses on platforms millions of people use every day on what we might term 'the main street of the internet'. Typing 'creepshot' into Twitter brings up images and videos of women going about their lives completely unaware of the camera lens trailing them. The first hit I get is a tweet sharing multiple images of a woman in gym gear waiting at a cross walk who had no idea she was being watched or that these images of her exist online. The next is a video of a woman in a bikini on the beach, having a conversation with another woman, oblivious to the camera lingering on her bum, her legs, her hips. The third is of a woman in a department store trying on sunglasses while someone behind her films her from the waist down, focusing on her bum. It is posted on an account dedicated to 'candid' shots of women and girls in public spaces all over the world, who are filmed and photographed unaware while shopping, walking down the street, socialising. Scrolling through the results, I'm reminded of moments in the gym when the sight of a smartphone in the hand of a man close by has set me on edge. I usually tell myself I'm being too sensitive, that he's just checking a message or putting on a podcast because most people – thankfully – do not behave this way, but looking at all these images, I'm realise I can't be sure. This is a digital world where the male gaze not only looks at women in everyday life but can now take what it sees, store it, distribute it, giving it ever greater control with little fear of consequence and few ways for victims to strike back.

Back in the seventies the feminist scholar Laura Mulvey described how classic Hollywood cinema's male gaze presented its dominance as a natural consequence of the power differentials between genders.[9] As John Berger put it, men act and women appear, underscoring how visual culture depicted the agency of men and the passivity of women as the inevitable order of things. Mulvey argued that in film the male characters and the audience (also positioned as male) projected their desires and fantasies onto images of women who could not return this gaze or speak back to it. These female characters were subjected to an intense, objectifying form of surveillance she terms 'fetishistic scopophilia' that attempts to control the object it is so deeply attracted to. Female characters who fail to comply find themselves outcast or dead, humiliated or otherwise violently disposed of. The 'visual pleasure' Mulvey refers to in the title of her famous essay on the male gaze always comes at the expense of female characters who are both what it desires and what it destroys. In the digital age, this kind of visual pleasure has taken on new forms, but its aims remain the same.

Online as offline, images of the feminine body and the masculine body circulate very differently. While masculine bodies can be interpreted in any number of ways, the feminine body struggles to transcend its cultural status as a sexual object.[10] Even when photographs of women are taken without their consent or distributed in ways they never intended, the expectation remains that they are the ones at fault for failing to predict and prevent the online abuse of their image. This shows just how deep-rooted assumptions about female complicity remain: even when women are unaware of being watched or how their image will end up being used, they are still somehow responsible for the consequences of deviant male behaviour. The irony is that this misuse of digital technologies proves what victims have been shouting for millennia, namely just how misogynistic some men are and the lengths they will go to to exert control over women known and unknown to them. These attacks are what communications professor Emma A. Jane calls a 'litmus test' for misogyny that has not gone away, persisting and indeed flourishing out of sight.[11]

In online abuse, digital technologies extend the capabilities of the male gaze to intimidate and discipline women, especially those it construes as stepping out of line. Women in the public eye have always had to deal with this type of sexism but the internet adds an additional, burdensome dimension. Research on female politicians and online abuse, for example, has revealed how social media makes them especially vulnerable to misogynist and racist intimidation. According to Amnesty International, in the six months before the 2017 UK general election, 25,000 abusive tweets were sent to female MPs.[12] Shockingly, one woman received almost a third of all those tweets: Labour's Diane Abbott, the first black woman elected to the British Parliament and the longest-serving black MP in British government. Describing what has changed since the eighties when she was first elected to enable such levels of abuse, Abbott told Amnesty International:

> When I was a new Member of Parliament, you might get one racist letter a week. But that was because if you were racist and you wanted to abuse an MP, you had to write a letter, you had to put it in

> an envelope, you had to put a stamp on it and you had to put it in the letter box. Now, some days, we can get hundreds of items of abuse, depending on what happened the previous day.[13]

Seyi Akiwowo is founder and CEO of Glitch,[14] a UK-based charity dedicated to ending gender-based online abuse. When I speak to Seyi over Skype, she points to stats on Twitter released by Amnesty International in 2018 showing that, in an analysis of 228,000 tweets sent to 778 women politicians and journalists based in the US and the UK, black women were 84 per cent more likely than white women to be mentioned in 'abusive or problematic' tweets.[15] Seyi has also experienced the effects of this reality first-hand, founding Glitch after a video of a speech she gave at a youth event in Strasbourg attracted the ire of neo-Nazis. 'I was on the receiving end of horrific trolling and abuse,' she says. 'But being a black woman back in 2017 when this happened, there was little conversation, support or resources.' This lack of resources motivated Seyi to found Glitch, one of the first organisations of its kind, whose mission focuses on awareness, advocacy and action. Glitch works with a range of stakeholders including tech companies and governments to build 'long-term systemic change'. But it's not just about large institutions. Instead of scrolling by, Seyi emphasises the need for individuals to be 'active bystanders online', by reporting abuse and supporting those affected. She uses the term 'digital citizens', which underscores the idea of social media as a public space of rights and responsibilities. Central to Glitch's work is an intersectional approach to ending online abuse; one that recognises how the intersections of women's identities, like race, gender and class, impact their ability to safely access online spaces.

'If we don't look at it through an intersectional lens, we're only going to make the online space safe for a small group of people who are in power or who are privileged, therefore enabling them to cause further damage and harm to those that are invisible, who don't have a platform,' Seyi explains:

> If you don't look at the world through an intersectional lens, you are missing out on how disabled women are facing abuse, you're missing out on how gifs are used to spark an epileptic attack for women with epilepsy; you're missing out on women in precarious employment who are facing online abuse and who are unable to speak out about how the online space impacts them. Sadly, we have to wait for these issues to affect white women, celebrities and entertainers before institutions start doing something about it.

When high-profile women like Abbott are relentlessly attacked online, it sends a message to every woman watching. That message is a warning about what to expect if you dare stick your head above the digital parapet: a warning that has little to do with the cut and thrust of politics or public life and everything to do with attempting to lock women out of access to power on the basis of their gender or race, not their ability or their ideas. This can make claiming visibility a tricky endeavour for women, especially if they are not shy about expressing themselves or talking back to the male gaze rather than acquiescing to it.

It's no surprise that social media has become a focal point for twenty-first-century feminist activism. When it comes to equality, much remains to be done and platforms such as Twitter provide accessible spaces for would-be changemakers to congregate. But as much as it is useful for expressing feminist ideas and feminist organising, social media visibility also makes activists and their activities open to those who want nothing more than to derail and abuse feminists.[16] Nowhere is this truer than in the most depraved parts of what is referred to as the anti-feminist manosphere, a world of incels (involuntary celibates), pick-up artists and proud misogynists exemplified by forums like Reddit's The Red Pill. Writer Angela Nagle describes this environment as one where there is 'a pretty relentless flow of sexual frustration, anxiety about evolutionary rank and foaming-at-the-mouth misogyny full of descriptions of women as "worthless cunts", "attention whores", "riding the cock carousel" and so on'.[17]

Many of those active on these sites do not just want to challenge or ridicule women, they want them to vacate the internet entirely. At the very least, the blossoming of these misogynistic cultures impacts women's ability to access these new digital public spaces, to participate in online life and to express themselves. At the worst, it causes emotional and/or physical harm, reputational damage and what Emma A. Jane calls 'economic vandalism',[18] where women miss out on career opportunities, cannot work or are forced to retreat from the internet, harming them financially (see careers in journalism for example, which have become increasingly reliant on building an online profile while at the same time women journalists and those from minorities face disproportionate levels of online abuse).[19] On the internet, harassment is archived and circulated; it becomes a spectacle, prolonging the suffering of those on the receiving end of it. Tackling it is far from straightforward because while technologies have developed rapidly, attitudes and the law often have not, leaving women to fight their corner with blunted tools that are built for the offline rather than the online world.

Victims' ability to fight back against online abuse isn't helped by well-intentioned but ineffective advice like 'don't feed the trolls', which often stems from the still-held belief that online abuse is somehow less harmful than its offline equivalent. This assumption was always unhelpful but never more so than now as we rely to an even greater degree on digital technology for everything from work to socialising to keeping in touch with our family and friends. The binary between 'offline' and 'online' is dissolving; for many young people it barely exists. While not feeding the trolls may work in cases where someone is just making a nuisance of themselves, for orchestrated, concentrated and sustained abuse it puts the onus on victims ahead of perpetrators. Not responding to rape threats may deny trolls the oxygen they crave but it does little to assuage women's fears about the potential viability of a threat. It also does nothing whatsoever to counterbalance an abuser's ability to exploit the internet and social media for their own ends, against an individual woman's inability to strike back.

What makes the modern-day internet so enjoyable is how it fosters interactivity, creativity and collaboration: it is a vibrant, image-driven space that appeals to our desire to see the world and share our slice of it. But abusers and trolls exploit this interconnectedness to increase their own visibility (emboldened by anonymity) in response to women's growing presence in these spaces. If one has the time or the inclination, it is easy to create dozens of anonymous accounts across numerous platforms to better attack victims and dodge bans or send reams of automated, abusive emails. If one so desires, it is also easy to set up basic websites for no other reason than to host malicious or damaging information about a target, with the aim of it being atop the search results whenever someone googles them. For those with even the most basic technological nous, avoiding your location being traced using virtual private networks (VPNs) is relatively straightforward. A modern-day misogynist can set off a metaphorical but potentially devastating bomb into a woman's life without ever having to leave his bed or his basement.

A number of years ago I interviewed an activist from the US called Annmarie about her experience in the early 2010s with what was then known as revenge porn but has since become more accurately termed 'image-based sexual abuse' or IBSA. While this form of abuse can happen to anyone, overwhelmingly it impacts women, often as an extension of intimate partner abuse[20] that takes place within a relationship or in its aftermath. Where revenge porn sounds salacious, performative and may even infer a degree of consent, image-based sexual abuse centres on the desire to harm and humiliate victims, placing this kind of behaviour on a continuum[21] of male violence against women and girls that has a long history.

This continuum is something women like Annmarie know all too well. Although much time has passed, the story she told about her treatment at the hands of a vindictive ex still chills me, illustrating how brutal but effective the tools of the internet can be for someone hell-bent on ruining a woman's life. Not only did this man post her naked images online, he posted them with her full name, home address and place of work, alongside a solicitation for sex. Annmarie effectively became a prisoner in her own home, terrified to leave or to answer the door. Her ex also submitted her images to porn sites and tried numerous times to auction a CD of her nude photos. As is so often the case when it comes to image-based abuse, the local police were of little help. Without strong laws at that time there was little, legally speaking, they could do and no way for her to press charges; they also lacked sensitivity in their handling of the situation, resulting in Annmarie feeling victim-blamed. The horror of the experience was such that it drove her to attempt suicide.

In the years since I corresponded with Annmarie, more jurisdictions have enacted laws to tackle the rise of image-based abuse. Ireland's new laws came into effect in February 2021 while in the UK it has been a criminal offence to share images without a subject's permission since 2015. There is also a growing awareness at an educational level that conversations around sex and consent need to be extended to include ethical considerations around the sharing of private images beyond their intended recipient. After countless hacking scandals highlighting how easily private information can be stolen, digital security is also something people from all walks of life are being urged to take much more seriously, from using strong passwords to thinking carefully about what to share online. While this is an improvement, there is no room for complacency. Many victims of image-based abuse still cannot access specific supports to deal with a crime of this nature. This includes mental-health services to cope with the emotional fallout, legal assistance to help file complaints (along with police officers who are trained to understand the impact of image-based abuse) and technological help to get their images taken down.

In 2020, as more people switched from offline living to being extremely online, rates of image-based abuse around the world skyrocketed. Australia alone recorded a 210 per cent increase in reports of image-based abuse between March and May 2020 compared to the same timeframe in the previous year.[22] For some victims, this initial violation is only the beginning of the nightmare.

'A friend of mine ended up on Pornhub. Her iCloud account was hacked and videos of her and her ex-partner were taken and uploaded with her full name attached. She was under eighteen at the time.' Kate Isaacs is the founder of the UK-based #NotYourPorn[23] campaign. Started in 2019, it fights to stop the online porn industry from circulating and profiting from image-based sexual abuse. Kate started the campaign after seeking support for her friend only to find it didn't exist:

> There was nothing essentially that we could do because the existing revenge-porn laws in England and Wales don't apply to the commercialised porn industry, which I just thought was absolutely wild. The perpetrator would be breaking the law for uploading that content to Pornhub, but Pornhub actively profiting from it – showcasing it, putting it in their categories and advertising it, which they were doing – wasn't against the law at all.

Over the phone, Kate tells me that the more she dug into the issue, the more horrified she became. Far from her friend's experience being an isolated one, she discovered numerous women who'd had similar experiences: 'It wasn't just a weird fluke that happened to my friend. There's entire genres on these porn sites dedicated to image-based abuse and non-consensual pornography. It was just horrifying. It was just one of those things where I couldn't believe it had been going on this entire time.' #NotYourPorn was born out of a desire to help and to sound the alarm:

> I just felt that this was an entire area that hadn't been tapped into and wasn't taken seriously. A big part of it is that someone has abused your right to consent in a sexual way so that's sexual abuse. That's one element of it which is fundamentally disgusting but there were these added layers on top that just made me feel incredibly sick. The fact that victims were experiencing abuse in such a public way by people who felt entitled to view that because it was up on the porn website; this entitlement to witness their abuse I thought was just horrifying. The other layer is that it was being profited from and it had been packaged up as porn.

Talking to Kate makes it clear how unaccountable sites like Pornhub are, not just in the UK but globally. This lack of accountability is something that has received little attention in the mainstream media until quite recently, possibly down to the fact that people are still uncomfortable talking about the industry. But while people may not be talking about porn, they are certainly consuming it: Pornhub alone had 42 billion visits in 2019.[24] The discomfort around discussing the issue belies the immense reach and influence of what is a vast but unregulated business. Part of the Mindgeek porn empire, Pornhub is frequently ranked alongside Google and Facebook as one of the most powerful websites in the world.[25] In 2019 the site received 115 million visits every twenty-four hours, the equivalent to, as its 'Insights' section puts it, 'the populations of Canada, Australia, Poland and the Netherlands all visiting in one day!'[26]

In December 2020 a damning *New York Times* op-ed entitled 'The Children of Pornhub' caused an international outcry.[27] The article chronicles the experiences of (mainly) young women, many of them victims of image-based abuse, whose images ended up on the site against their will while they were underage, producing devastating effects that altered the course of their lives. As with Kate's friend, many of those interviewed struggled to get their images taken down. In the aftermath of the piece, Pornhub disabled its download button, which had allowed users to save and upload images again and again, even after they had been removed.[28] When Visa and Mastercard blocked the use of their cards on the site in response to the *New York Times* piece, Pornhub pledged to remove all unverified material from the site. This resulted in 80 per cent of its content being taken down practically overnight.[29]

'Removing 80 per cent of their content is a big deal,' says Kate. 'Although we welcome that, it's also bittersweet. It took a major credit card company pulling out and not victims' pleas.' Pointing out how reliant Pornhub and similar companies are on material that is pirated or stolen, she adds, 'We cannot trust this porn company, or any of these porn companies, to self-regulate.'

Reflecting on the impact on victims, Kate explains that the lack of understanding around image-based abuse causes many to retreat into silence:

> In the beginning, I was like, why is nobody talking about this? But if you've already had your consent

> taken away and [been] put out there so publicly, why would anyone shout about it? You want it to go away, you want to pull it [your image/s] down as quickly as possible. There's so much shame associated with it. Victims are essentially voiceless. And if they do speak about it, they are massively victim-blamed. I feel we have moved on in terms of physical and sexual abuse: the majority of us don't ask questions such as what she was wearing, but in this case, and when it comes to digital sexual abuse, there seems to be a wall. People feel it's a virtual world and it's not real.

When I ask Kate how her friend is doing now, her answer illustrates the long shadow this abuse casts over victims' lives:

> As soon as something's uploaded, they don't moderate it. It can be downloaded hundreds of thousands of times, which means that even if they remove it in five minutes that could have been shared and that lives on the internet forever. I think for her, she goes through waves of thinking, OK it's gone, no one is talking about it anymore. But then she also has to live with the fact that whoever she comes into contact with, whoever she dates, if she has children in the future, anyone could view that of her. Everyone has access to her in that sexual way. For her, that was completely soul-destroying.

'This morning I received an unsolicited dick pic via @ Instagram from a man I do not know. What follows is a beautiful story I wove about an app I made up, that should exist. Enjoy!'

So begins a post by Jenn Tisdale, explaining the genesis of a fictional app she christened the 'Cockblock', which she dreamt up to bait the man who sent her the unsolicited image in question. Upon receipt of the picture of his member she pretended to him that she could not see it, thanks to her Cockblock app which is, she tells him, 'very useful for women'. Realising something is not quite right, Tisdale's would-be wooer backpedals, claiming the picture was a punchline to a 'really shitty joke'. Tisdale goes on to describe the app as 'very intuitive', explaining that it immediately sends the image and any identifying details to the police, who then invite her to make a sexual harassment report: 'Men who have sent me dick pics have been arrested. LOL, one guy even lost his job and his wife. Technology is wild.'[30]

I saw Tisdale's post because it was regrammed on @ byefelipe,[31] an Instagram account with half a million followers renowned for its screenshot collection of horrendous online dating encounters. The page is very funny but also depressing, cataloguing a digital world where age-old objectification piggybacks on the access provided by social media to demean and harass women. While much of the material posted to @byefelipe is so ridiculous it's hard to see it as anything other than pathetic, it showcases an alarming amount of male entitlement and attitudes to gender roles that would be right at home in the fifties. While pathetic, many of the posts on @byefelipe also have an air of menace; others are outright expressions of violent desires. Taking Tisdale's experience, image-based abuse most often refers to images shared of women without their consent, but it could also apply to images of a sexual nature that are *sent* to individuals without their consent. These images are, after all, intrusive and sometimes upsetting, demanding a woman's attention to the degree that addressing their inappropriateness becomes her problem rather than the problem of the man who sent it. But while flashing one's genitals at strangers is illegal in the offline world, dick-pic senders are subject to no such constraints. This sense of impunity is especially striking in the worst posts on @byefelipe, as if the 'real world' of law, consequence and basic civility is some far-off imaginary. In one particularly nasty example, a man calls a woman fat, threatens to beat her to death, adding in a twisted expression of desire, 'let me lick you though'. Thanks to dating apps, expressing these sorts of sentiments directly to women has never been easier and it is no surprise that sexual violence linked to app use is becoming a serious issue.[32] Creeps with vicious tongues are not confined to nightclubs or streets anymore: under the guise of romance they can now get into women's heads, wherever they are, with just a couple of clicks.

For as long as the internet existed in its modern format, people have used it to find love. The first online dating site, Kiss.com, went live in 1994. With the rise of social media, the stigma once associated with online dating has all but disappeared. This has produced a thriving digital dating industry in a world where dating apps have become a normal way to meet someone. They are also a huge global business. Launched in 2012, Tinder is the biggest of them all, with 57 million users worldwide. To give an idea of the scale involved, there are an estimated *one million* Tinder dates every week and 1.6 billion swipes on the app *per day*.[33] But what's good for business might not be so good for human relationships or for equality.

Apps such as Tinder have been criticised for gamifying dating, turning it into a festival of notification 'dings', endless choice and compulsive swiping in the hope of the next match being better than the last.[34] This turns the pursuit of romance into something akin to distractedly skimming a never-ending shopping catalogue in search of a better deal. Tinder in particular places a huge emphasis on one's image, where a person's profile has little to do with their interests and dreams, and everything to do with how they look. Researchers found that this environment increases appearance pressures, which can manifest in negative perceptions about one's body and image.[35] These can become internalised, driving people to compare themselves, often harshly, with others. When this competitive, dehumanising process meets with the dehumanisation that is inherent to objectification, enmeshed in a culture where the emphasis is on casual sex rather than long-term commitment, it is not difficult to see why dating apps have become a breeding ground for harassment. This is reflected in findings such as those produced by the Pew Research Centre in the United States in 2020, which found that 57 per cent of female online dating users aged 18 to 24 had been sent a 'sexually explicit message or image they did not ask for'.[36] Pew also found that 'Younger female users are also about twice as likely as their male counterparts to say someone on a dating site or app has called them an offensive name (44 per cent vs 23 per cent) or threatened to physically harm them (19 per cent vs 9 per cent).'[37]

Researching this chapter, I put a call out on my Twitter to ask women about their less-than-great experiences with dating apps. Harriet, a lecturer in the UK, gets in touch to tell me about a man she met on a dating app who we will call 'Steve'. While messaging for a few days before meeting, she and Steve appeared to have lots in common. 'He seemed pleasant, smart, funny, all the usual things,' she wrote over email. 'He claimed to also like my favourite cartoon so there was a mutual interest.' As you do, Harriet arranged to meet Steve for a coffee as a first date. As soon as he arrived, things veered into the strange. Steve bought her 'unusual' gifts: lip balm, a T-shirt of a character from the cartoon they both watched and, most unsettlingly, underwear that Harriet describes as 'big unsexy pants'. This was all made even more unnerving by his insistence on sitting right next to her in the coffee shop as opposed to across the table, as you normally would when meeting someone for the first time.

It was immediately clear that things such as boundaries and how intimacy works were not Steve's strong points. Understandably, Harriet was keen to leave. 'I politely excused myself after gulping my coffee and was hoping to get away with a polite but firm message later to say no thanks,' she said:

> Nope. He messaged me fifty-five times in the time it took me to get home (twenty minutes) and when I blocked him, he decided to use my work email and phone (which are easy to find) to send bizarre messages. Some sexual, some references to the cartoon. He also sent me a lot of photos of the building in which I work, which I immediately reported because it felt threatening. In one he was topless in the foreground with the building behind him.

Steve is representative of so many dating-app horror stories where charming online personas crumble in the daylight. While this can be annoying whatever your gender, the rise of violence and harassment relating to dating apps makes it a particularly dangerous issue for women. The simple truth is that it can be hard to get an accurate sense of a person over an app. When someone is physically present, you can better observe their body language and their tone; it's far from failsafe but it can be a more useful indicator of someone's personality and intentions. Online, our senses cannot do their job properly because we are dealing with screens. In safety terms, Harriet did everything right: meeting in a public space, not hanging around when she felt uncomfortable, but it was no match for Steve's persistence. It is of course ridiculous that a grown man should behave this way. His entitlement is matched only by his staggering inability to understand and respect simple social expectations and dating decorum. But as much as Steve's antics are daft, they are also intrusive, intimidating and excessive. Harriet tells me he only stopped contacting her once she got the police involved.

The emphasis that dating-app culture puts on casual sex creates an environment where women are presumed to be sexually available by virtue of simply being visible on the app, even when women's profiles state they are seeking a relationship. In these spaces, what women want is often beside the point. Whatever the case, she will be judged by bad actors as a frigid or a slattern or potentially both because her sexuality online, as offline, is regarded as not hers to define. This makes it difficult for women to set boundaries around what constitutes appropriate behaviour because the men who take their presence on dating apps as evidence of their being 'up for it' use the app's functionality to make their assumptions and desires clear. This process turns women into objects in their eyes, rendering what a woman wants immaterial.

Eve is a bit of a dating-app veteran. When I tell her about this book, she offers to speak to me, beginning with the story of one Juan, who appeared to be a very good-looking Spaniard but probably wasn't. After connecting with Juan on an app and spending a few days messaging him, Eve decided to give him her number. She quickly regretted it. 'As soon as he got my number, the dick pics started,' she sighs, adding that Juan also introduced her to the concept of sex gifs, which he interspersed with his dick pics. 'When I think about it now, of course there's sex gifs – I just wasn't sending them or looking them up,' she laughs, grimacing. 'It was the first time in my dating life that happened. I was kind of like, oh my God, that's not me, but I did not know this guy, had not met him, and here he was sending me dick pics.'

Initially Eve tried to be an up-for-it woman, an archetype that is so visible across popular culture, the kind that wouldn't be fazed by a dick pic or ten:

> There was one day I remember, I picked up my phone and I thought, I'll give him a chance. I can be that girl. I could just meet him for drinks. I could just have sex with him and I can walk away. I don't know who I was trying to convince because that's just not me. I messaged him and I was like, hey Juan, how's it going? How are you? It was one o'clock in the day and he messaged back with a dick pic. I'll never forget it.

She duly sent Juan on his merry way but two years later, the experience has stayed with her:

> I don't think there's any girl out there, and I mean this genuinely, who enjoys getting dick pics. Let's face it, they're not the most beautiful thing in the world to look at. I felt violated. It made me feel

> things about myself like, oh he didn't have enough respect for me. Obviously, we didn't know each other, but he didn't have enough respect to not send me a dick pic or ask my consent. A man who I had never met … I had a picture of his penis on my phone. It's disgusting when you think about it. It's massively disturbing.

In 2019 Tinder made revenue in the region of $1.15 billion.[38] As the online dating industry grows, heightened now by the switch to online living and romancing during the pandemic, dating apps use a variety of ways to get cash from users. These include apps that are pay-to-use and paid tiers, which are meant to be more selective than the free versions of apps. For many women, one of the appeals of paid services is the hope that they will provide a more select match: men less inclined to send unsolicited dick pics or a barrage of sleazy messages, for example. But as Eve's experience shows, paying platforms in the hope of avoiding the Juans of this world doesn't necessarily work. 'I think there is this notion out there that if you pay for a dating app, that means you get rid of all the creeps,' she says. 'That is 100 per cent not true because unfortunately sociopathic men can afford to pay for dating apps too.' She tells me about signing up for a pay-to-use dating app and the let-down that quickly followed:

> I paid sixty or eighty quid to subscribe and I woke up to a message from a man saying 'fuck me'. And again, I thought, is it something about me that men think they can do that, even though it was nothing about me and all about them? But my thinking at the time was, what am I doing to attract this, that

> a man thinks it's okay to send me a message saying 'fuck me'?

Eve contacted the app's complaints department and although they were responsive, she cancelled her subscription soon afterwards.

In Eve's experience, women generally use dating apps in the hope of meeting someone while men generally use them with the expectation of no-strings-attached sex, a perspective I have heard echoed many times. As someone who works in a public role, Eve often finds these kinds of men sliding into her DMs on Facebook, leaving messages along the lines of 'tie me up'. 'You're just like, ugh, these men on the internet – and it was sent at two o'clock in the morning,' she says, sounding tired and resigned:

> *Tie me up, fuck me*, all these things, intimate things. If you're a couple and you're into that sort of stuff, that's all well and good, but to send that to an absolute stranger that you've never met? Every single time I was on my own when I got one of those messages and every single time, it made me feel so horrible about myself. Dirty, almost.

Dating apps and social media make us more visible and accessible to others than we otherwise would be. While this certainly has its positives, it can make individuals vulnerable to those who use the surveillance these platforms normalise to enact abuse. For women caught in damaging relationships with an ex or current partner, or who find themselves the object of unwanted attention, this vulnerability can put them in tremendous danger. This danger can be physical, but it can also be emotional and psychological, a combination that straddles both the online and offline worlds. Abuse from current or former partners or the unwanted attentions of strangers is far from new, but what is new is how social media allows abusers to extend and intensify their presence in their victims' lives. As far back as the early 2010s researchers found that cyberstalking, for example, had become more prevalent than its offline counterpart.[39] In May 2020, just two months into the pandemic, UK anti-stalking charities and the police reported a surge in contact from those worried about cyberstalking.[40] The cruel irony was that the same technology many people were relying on to work and stay in contact was being used as a tool of abuse against women who were already severely isolated. A statement from the Suzy Lamplugh Trust, which runs a national stalking helpline in the UK, said the surge in cyberstalking focused on social media, email and messaging apps.[41] Technologies that were a source of comfort for so many had become, in the hands of abusers, a source of terror for the already vulnerable at a time of personal and national crisis.

While one might assume that the physical constraints of lockdown would give stalking victims in the physical world a reprieve, experts warn this is not necessarily the case. This is especially true online, where the distance between perpetrators and their victims is not bound by geography or locked doors. This allows perpetrators to have an impact on victims even when they are separated, making it incredibly difficult for women to feel safe or to contemplate escape. In this scenario, it seems as if the abuser is omnipresent.

A report by the BBC on the surge of cyberstalking complaints during the lockdown shows the degree to which determined abusers can exploit technology to violate their victims. Entitled 'Stalking: my ex-partner sent me 4000 emails', the report details the case of a woman's ex who had pleaded guilty to stalking her – using social media to endlessly contact her after they broke up – threatening to kill himself and begging forgiveness.[42] The intensity of the contact was staggering. In addition to the 4000 emails, her ex made in the region of 300 phone calls and text messages numbering in the hundreds. She described being 'hounded and persecuted at every point, on a daily basis, many times a day' and how her ex contacted her on 'any platform where I was reachable' including her PayPal. In a statement the victim, who was not named, described the emotional impact this had on her and her family:

> Just because the messages were not direct threats or harmful doesn't mean it cannot have the same emotional impact ... I have had to change my whole life to ensure that my children and I were kept safe throughout this. I still have to maintain this, and my life will never be the same again.[43]

Exercising power over victims has always been regarded as a core motivation in domestic violence and intimate partner abuse. This desire is expressed not only physically but also through emotional and psychological harm. In the last few years there has been a growing awareness of the impact of coercive control, which Women's Aid defines as 'a persistent pattern of controlling, coercive and threatening behaviour including all or some forms of domestic abuse, emotional, physical, financial, sexual (including threats) by a boyfriend, partner, husband or ex'.[44] This type of abuse is so pernicious because it can be hard to describe and articulate, making it difficult for women trapped by these relationships to leave or get the support they so badly need. As technology has become deeply interwoven with every aspect of everyday life, its affordances or what it enables people to do have been used by abusers to access their victims, giving rise to phenomena such as 'technology facilitated coercive control' and 'intimate partner surveillance'. This control is exercised through activities like social media harassment, email hacking, 'doxing' (the publishing of private information online), using spyware to monitor phones and computers and sending threatening messages. Innocent actions on social media – tagging someone in an image or 'checking in' at one's location – can be utilised by abusers to monitor and stalk victims. One research paper describes an online forum dedicated to intimate partner surveillance where members swap tips and techniques and share their experiences of surveilling a partner.[45] Now, without ever leaving their homes or being physically present with their victims, abusers can toy with them through the internet and use it to glean information about their activities offline, and they can find community with those similarly minded. This adds another dimension to the already horrific reality of domestic and intimate partner abuse, where digital technology is used to harass victims online and offline, compounding the harms women and their dependents are already subject to.

Reading about the experiences of those who have experienced gender-based abuse via technology, one is struck by how suffocating it can be, as if one's abuser is somehow everywhere even if they are physically absent and the relationship is over. Writing about her experience in the context of the website Broadly's 'UnfollowMe' investigation into domestic violence and stalking in the UK, journalist Nana Baah compares the tropes of romantic comedies to the obsessions of her ex who stalked her via social media.[46] What romantic comedies depict as 'the chase' – that cheeky guy who just won't take 'no' for an answer! – was in fact harassment.

Baah describes how the abuse developed after a break-up when the man she once found charming began to exhibit a much darker side. To get around her blocking him on Facebook, her ex created an alternative account with the same profile picture but a different name. Baah didn't respond to his friend request but he kept messaging. This went on for months, veering from the apologetic to abusive until she finally blocked him, a move that should have been enough but wasn't. Things escalated further when he began setting up multiple 'anonymous' Instagram accounts to contact her, using terminology specific to their time together. Baah writes that she 'felt sick' every time she received a message from him. Following the standard advice, she repeatedly blocked him, to little avail. Contacting the police, she was told there was not much they could do aside from asking him to stop. So long as he denied the messages were coming from him, the police said their hands were tied. As is so often the case given the lack of legal mechanisms to properly tackle online abuse, the internet seemed to be empowering Baah's abuser at the expense of his victim.

After contacting the police, Baah didn't hear from her abuser for eight months but that didn't mean he wasn't still in her head. She writes: 'I always thought he was going to come back; I was waiting for the next account to pop up.'[47] In time he did, circulating rumours about her offline and trying to contact her online. For Baah, her ex's actions reflected his desire to violate her privacy at an emotional and psychological level. It was not enough to simply use the technology to watch her; he wanted her to *know* he was doing so, a reality that kept her in a state of fear while he used the power granted to him by social media to repeatedly violate her boundaries.

Accounts such as those of the victim in the BBC's report and Baah's show just how effectively abusers can harness the visibility and accessibility of social media to prey upon their targets. What compounds the harm in cases like these are cultural attitudes, which assume because online abuse happens on the internet rather than 'real life', it doesn't harm individuals in the way that actual physical violence does. What these attitudes reflect is firstly a lack of understanding for how abuse occurs; in any context, it does not have to be physical to harm victims profoundly. Secondly, it shows no appreciation for the way offline and online lives now bleed into one another, and how an offline abuser can use digital tools to intensify and extend his terrorising of his victim so that she feels as unsafe on social media as she does in her own home. Thirdly, it overlooks how real these experiences are to the women who are on the receiving end of them. We live in a world where violence against women is everywhere when it comes to entertainment and popular culture yet sidelined when it comes to properly funded resources and supports for victims. Dismissing online abuse stems from the same root as dismissing offline abuse; a suspicion that women are being 'hysterical' or making it up, culminating in a refusal to acknowledge how debilitating the spectre of violence can be. This can culminate in tragedies where abuse is acknowledged only when it is too late.

Digital technology may make communication simpler and faster than ever before but it also gifts harassers and abusers multiple ways to contact their victims at will and repeatedly. As Diane Abbott pointed out, this style of communication is not constrained like the hate mail of the past, which took time to write, post and deliver; digital technology has cut the space between writing and receipt down to seconds, the inbox and DMs providing more space for malicious messages than its offline precursor, the modest mailbox, could ever accommodate. In this landscape, blocking, filtering and reporting these communications only goes so far, as does getting the police involved. What victims are left with is a digital realm that has revolutionised communication, one that errs on the side of free expression at the expense of policing actions that are illegal in the offline world (hello, dick pics); a broader culture that still does not take such abuse sufficiently seriously; and a legal system struggling to play catch-up.

If an abuser wants to be persistent. they can create a new account or a new alias or a new email address, a process that takes only minutes and requires things most people have at their disposal, such as a phone and a Wi-Fi connection. The onus thus falls on the victim to reduce and manage their visibility, changing email addresses repeatedly, shutting their Instagram and Facebook or forgoing social media entirely. This may starve abusers of the information they crave but it can also isolate victims further, prohibiting them from enjoying the benefits and freedoms of online life that their predator has weaponised for their own sick games. But even this may not be enough for some abusers, who will use the surveillance capacities of the internet to sniff out even the faintest digital footprint left by their victims.

@Instagranniepants is an Instagram account full of highly amusing artwork.[48] The aim of the page is an interesting one: 'Objectifying men who objectify women in 3 easy steps: Man sends crude line via internet. Draw him naked. Send portrait to lucky man, enjoy results.' The page's creator, Anna Gensler, is a talented artist who uses her skills to depict men who misbehave on dating apps in the nip, looking rather deflated. Simple but effective. So we meet Leo who called his prospective date a 'stuck up bitch' and Austin, who calls the object of his affection 'a bitch' with a 'shitty cunt personality' who would 'probably like a dick in your ass anyway'. And who could forget Luke, who charmed his prospective date with this proposition: 'My friend is having an orgy tonite [sic]. I need a partner. Condom and lube provided. Oral + vag sex only. Won't be that bad.'

Like @byefelipe, it's hard not to laugh at the childish vileness of the posts on @Instagranniepants and the sheer audacity of those who use dating apps to send such grotesque material to strangers. If you want to secure a date, this really doesn't seem to be the way to go about it, but then perhaps a date isn't the point: the dark thrill of accessing and getting a reaction out of a woman is. The entitlement on display and the casual way threats of sexual violence are thrown about make one feel that some of these men will need a lot more than a humiliating picture foisted in their direction to make them rethink their approach. While the material is funny, it is also unsettling. Laughter can certainly be a form of resistance (just ask the feminists who crowned a sheep in protest at the 1969 Miss America contest), a refusal to let bad actors invade one's mind and sense of security by mocking as sad what they regard as imposing, sexually dominant behaviour. But laughter alone risks normalising what is abhorrent and unacceptable while potentially downplaying the discomfort women may feel about these kinds of messages, no matter how patently ridiculous their sender may be. To quote Margaret Atwood, 'Men are afraid women will laugh at them. Women are afraid men will kill them.'[49]

Misogyny is as old as humanity itself. Successive waves of feminism and an appreciation for equality as a social and political good may have softened its roar in some parts of the world, but the internet has revealed its persistence, offering new tools and a new terrain to stalk for those who feel justified in their hatred of women. Anonymity, combined with social isolation and a victimhood complex, can make a heady mix for those who feel that women owe them right of access. Although condemning this hatred is right, it is also imperative that we ask wider questions about why it is some men feel compelled to act this way and how the internet is potentially intensifying the disenfranchisement they feel.

Some of the answers to these questions are likely found in the changing economic landscape of the last forty years. This has seriously undermined the breadwinner model men are still encouraged to emulate despite declining wages and job security. Meanwhile, more women have entered the workforce, contributing to the (inaccurate) sense that women – rather than an ailing economic system – are to blame for declining opportunities. Add to this the kinds of 'philosophies' rife on sites like The Red Pill, which argue that changes in gender roles, specifically women's independence and ability to be more selective about their partner, has, in the minds of many men lurking in the netherworld of the manosphere, locked them out of the sexual marketplace.[50] Other answers can be found in cultural ideas that have remained resistant to revision, no matter what strides women make in public life or how clearly they make their case to be recognised and respected as thinking, feeling, and yes, sexual beings in their own right. Just as technology (and the law) needs to change to address the horrors of phenomena such as image-based abuse, so too do the culture and societies from which it springs.

The visibility that is social media's selling point can be weaponised by men who do not see women as equal but as targets and as objects, playthings for their gaze. No woman should have her life destroyed over a selfie she sends to her lover or a nude that is stolen from her phone, but in the world as it is, that is a real possibility. Talking to me about image-based abuse before Ireland's laws on the issue were finally enacted, the activist Megan Sims, herself a victim of the crimes she now campaigns against, emphasised the terror felt by those she tries to help: terror that their images will be released; terror that they already have been; terror that the rest of their lives, from finding a partner to having a career to even securing housing, is now an impossibility. The double standards that have always plagued women when it comes to sexual expression now extract a price that leaves them vulnerable in ways people outside the spaces Megan describes still struggle to understand. Yet, as she says, this is what is normal now; so normal, in fact, that health bodies across the world advised people to conduct their romantic liaisons via the internet during the pandemic.

Technology has changed how we love and how we are sexual. It has changed how we connect with potential partners and how abusers abuse. But it hasn't changed attitudes, nor has it in many countries changed the law – leaving far too many women at the mercy of sites and apps that make long-standing forms of shaming, judgement and harassment easier than ever to enact. We are told that these platforms represent progress, but too often they only intensify violations with which many women are already far too familiar.

And this begs the question: who exactly is benefiting from this so-called progress? Because when it comes to sexism and abuse, it certainly isn't women.

Six

Change

In 2018 young South Korean women began posting thousands of videos on social media of themselves destroying their make-up. In a country famous for high rates of plastic surgery (one-third of young Korean women are estimated to have gone under the knife)[1] and its elaborate, now globally popular K-Beauty regimes that can require ten steps or more, it was a bold rejection of the conservative status quo. The make-up protests are part of a growing feminist sentiment in the country that has culminated in what is now known as the 'Escape the Corset' movement, drawing parallels with restrictive clothing and restrictive ideas about femininity.[2] Make-up is not the only thing South Korean feminist activists reject: they cut their hair short and put on glasses, acts considered shocking in a society that expects women to embody a hyper-groomed, traditional and non-confrontational femininity. One young activist, Cha Ji-won, told *The Guardian*: 'There's only so much mental energy a person has each day, and I used to spend so much of it worrying about being "pretty". Now I use that time to read books and exercise.'[3]

The Escape the Corset movement is interesting on several levels. Firstly, it shows how activists can harness social media visibility to do political work, publicly defying powerful gazes that insist they must look a certain way to be valued as 'feminine'. Secondly, it shows how digital technologies enable the local and the global to collide, with the potential to provoke social change or at least, overdue conversations. In the case of South Korea, the impact of #MeToo since 2016, itself an internet phenomenon, led to widespread feminist organising, protests online and offline and an ongoing public reckoning for a technologically advanced but patriarchal culture in which women are still routinely paid less than men. While #MeToo began in the United States, its embrace by South Korean activists is rooted in experiences specific to their country. Among them is the murder of a 23-year-old woman at Gangnam train station, Seoul, in 2016 and the issue of *molka*, a form of high-tech voyeurism where victims (who are overwhelmingly women) are filmed in public (bathrooms, subways) and in private (their home, hotel rooms) and the videos shared online. Although a crime, laws against *molka* are notoriously ineffective, resulting in a little more than a slap on the wrist for perpetrators, while victims have little chance of getting their images off the internet once they are uploaded.[4]

It is hard not to be struck by the irony that, as demand for K-Beauty rockets in the West, many young Korean women are rethinking their relationship to make-up and the beauty industry in the context of broader issues of equality. Twenty-something Yuna is based in the UK but her family hails from South Korea and she visits regularly.

'A lot of my friends who grew up in Korea, they'll literally talk about, oh, before I escaped the corset, like a B.C. kind of thing,' she says of this shift. 'So many of them say, oh yeah, I used to wear so much make-up. Now there's actually a Korean expression, which is "no make-up face". It's really interesting that make-up has become such an expression of that change.'

Although some might dismiss this very public rejection of beauty standards as frivolous, in South Korea's male-dominated culture, it is not for the faint of heart. Activists risk alienating their families and prospective partners and diminishing their work prospects. Then there are the emotional costs. In a YouTube video by former South Korean plus-sized beauty blogger Lina Bae,[5] she takes the viewer through her make-up regime while the captions relay the cruel, contradictory comments she has received about her appearance. At the beginning, when she is barefaced, the captions urge her to put make-up on: 'your bare face is terror to my eyes lol'. When she does, applying foundation, eyeshadow, red lipstick and the rest, the comments change, this time telling her to 'make-up lightly', warning her that men don't appreciate women who wear too much make-up. In the final third of the video, Lina wipes her face clean, puts on her glasses, ties back her hair and smiles into the camera, tenderly holding her face in her hands. She glows but not in the way the cosmetic industry understands: this is about what is within, rather than without. The captions change again – now it is she, addressing the viewer directly, telling them, 'Don't be yourself who is made by others. Find your true colours. I will always support you.' At the time of writing, the video has been watched almost ten million times.

Escape the Corset is a site of many intersections. It illustrates the usefulness of social media as a political tool for activists and as a space for community-building in the face of adversity. But it is important to remember that this organising is motivated in part as a response to violations such as *molka*, itself a reflection of the how digital technology can be used to judge and shame women and how often this abuse is met with indifference at a cultural and legal level. This contradiction is at the heart of the visibility trap, where the benefits of social media are undermined by forces that use this new visibility to silence, abuse and intimidate. Visibility on these platforms can feel good and it can certainly be used to build activist networks but as we've seen throughout this book, it also makes users vulnerable to forces like surveillance and judgement, with little support when things go wrong. This begs the question of just how 'empowering' these platforms can really be expected to be. At the root of this issue is the urgent need for change on multiple fronts: change in individual behaviour, change in the law, change in technology and in attitudes, changes that collectively can help us reimagine our relationship to social media as it is and as it could be.

In 2018 virtual-reality pioneer and technology philosopher Jaron Lanier published the book *Ten Arguments for Deleting Your Social Media Accounts Right Now*.[6] Given his pedigree, Lanier's stance is interesting. Far from being a Luddite, he is someone who has a deep love for technology and the technology community, and a belief in its immense potential to do good. That potential, he argues, is not being realised in social media platforms as they exist today. Instead, users are left with little choice in the type of the platform they use, as all the major platforms – the ones where it feels as if everyone is hanging out – broadly follow the same profit model, based on surveillance, algorithmic manipulation and endless feedback loops. Lanier makes a strong case for why this creates a race to the bottom, where all that matters is the amount of attention given by users, not its benefits and certainly not its negatives.

Across his ten arguments to quit social media, Lanier warns that users are losing their free will, are being turned into 'assholes', are having the value of their words stripped and are losing their capacity for empathy, becoming unhappier in the process. Lanier sees social media as a core component in what he terms 'the insanity of our times', a force that is driving economic precariousness and 'making politics impossible'. Connecting the perpetual visibility of surveillance to human emotional states, he urges us to consider what plugging ourselves into the 'judgement machine' of social media is doing to our self-esteem levels. Lanier challenges us to think about the costs of letting others determine our worth and what we are losing by not having space within our lives where we can be ourselves, without being surveyed.

Lanier accepts that not everyone agrees with his stance but he sticks to it, saying he will be happy to be proved wrong if his warnings turn out to be unnecessary.[7] He acknowledges that not everyone is able to delete their social media – a reality that has become even more solidified in a post-pandemic world. But his recommendation that we get rid of our social media accounts in protest at the poor quality of the products currently on offer and their harms, and as a way to reclaim our minds and emotions, reminded me of scenarios I have encountered time and again in my work and amongst my peers and my friends. It also echoes in the experiences of influencers and content creators discussed in Chapter Four.

Usually it goes something like this: prompted by a period of dissatisfaction or a bad experience or overwhelm, a person quits or deletes a platform for a period of time that is long enough to be habit-forming (three weeks or more, generally speaking). Their absence from the platform provides space for critical reflection and a respite from the demands of visibility. If they return to that platform they often do so in ways that are more self-aware and selective than their previous engagement. Whereas before they may have let social media drift into their lives uncontested, now they approach it much more consciously. Over time, this enables them to establish a healthier engagement. They are not deleting their accounts in the exact way Lanier describes, nor is it equivalent to a 'digital detox' that applies to digital technologies in a broad sense. Rather, they use deleting or taking a break to reset their relationship to social media, to incorporate a fuller understanding of its impact on them and what, if anything, they are meaningfully using it for.

While researching this book I used social media for one thing it is truly great for: connecting us with people outside of our immediate network. In one of my call-outs I asked to speak to women who had taken a break from social media. The volume of responses set my researcher alarm bells ringing. Although not a scientific test, the number of those who got in touch to a single tweet to say they had taken a much-needed breather from certain social media sites opened my eyes to how individuals are trying to manage the effects of visibility in their lives. It also alerted me to actions such as those mentioned earlier that we undertake to create necessary emotional distance between ourselves and the social media we consciously choose to use, developing personalised approaches that serve the specific needs and interests of the individual, rather than the other way around.

One of the women I spoke with was Phoebe, a journalism student, who deactivated her Instagram account during a time when she was under pressure with college work and friendship problems. When she reactivated, something interesting happened. 'I don't use Instagram in the same way I did before,' she told me. 'I post much less; I watch much less. I keep seeing pieces about how you should treat Instagram like a magazine subscription and you should follow and unfollow what you want to see and not feel any pressure. I think I have a much healthier attitude to it now that I had that break away from it.'

What Phoebe describes is effectively hitting the reset button on how she uses Instagram, a process that for her meant a lengthy break. From those I've spoken with, this usually means a break of weeks or even months, either by deactivating or deleting your account with no 'logging in for a quick lurk'. Taking time away from the platform and then reworking how she used it when she returned provided relief from the pressures she had been feeling. Fundamental to this was, as Phoebe describes, using the platform much less, adjusting who she followed and being unapologetic about tailoring her use to her needs, not the demands of the platform or the expectations of her followers. Given her position as a trainee journalist, maintaining a presence makes sense for Phoebe as social media can be a super place to find stories and sources – but that is using it as a tool, rather than as a form of recreation.

Taking time away from social media also helped Jane, who works in the NGO sector, gain some clarity on behaviours that had been bothering her. 'I definitely feel better without it because I'm just way more mindful of what I'm consuming in terms of media,' she told me, discussing how she felt after closing her Instagram account:

> There were really strange things I noticed. I would save pictures or videos of recipes but I would never, ever make anything that I was saving. Never. I would just save it and feel like I'd done something when I hadn't. But then I've noticed recently that I've been doing way more things and it's not a false sense of achievement or connection.

For Jane, and Phoebe, creating emotional distance between her and her social media use enables her to use the technology more purposefully, gaining a greater degree of personal satisfaction in the long run. 'I don't miss it,' Jane said of Instagram:

> Once I stopped using it, I realised it just wasn't adding anything to my life. And I think you think that it is, and then you're like, what about all these people I'm following? How will I know what they're doing? But I found that if there were people I wanted to look up such as Beyoncé, I could when I had time. If I was being mindful about it and I wanted to read a story or look at a photo or whatever, I would look it up instead of just this constant stream of things that I thought I needed to see. When really, once you're out of it you're like, 'oh, I didn't actually need to look at a hundred different images before breakfast'. I just felt that I did.

In my research I use the term 'negotiating visibility' to refer to the way users try to achieve a level of visibility they feel is required and desirable on social media while attempting to mitigate any downsides. This can be a fraught balancing act, as many of the elements involved are beyond the individual user's control, most obviously the design of the platform not to mention who might be watching. This negotiation is an emotionally knotty affair, bound up in wanting to be seen and accepted while also wanting to avoid judgement in spaces where judgement can be triggered at any moment in a very public fashion and visibility makes everyone a potential target. Visibility, then, is closely tied to emotion and understanding how this works is vital to figuring out better ways to incorporate social media in its current form into our lives, should we need or want to do so.

On social media and elsewhere on the internet, the good and the grim intermingle in a kind of digital soup. It's the buzz we get when a tweet racks up a ton of likes that is immediately undercut when we realise the one or two individuals we really hoped would like it haven't. Ambivalence as a feeling is tricky: it's neither one thing nor the other, although it tends to veer towards the negative. With social media as it is designed today, users can have the good – but only if they put up with the bad and the *very* bad because they form inseparable parts of the same experience.[8] Internet scholars point out that while emotion plays a critical role online, there is still so much we don't understand about the interplay between our feelings and digital technology. What we do know suggests that online communication is no less powerful or complex than its offline counterpart (if such a dichotomy can be said to exist anymore), a point reflected in the emotional highs, but also in the lows, social media can elicit.

As someone who is paid to be professionally curious, I regularly ask people for their thoughts on the role social media now plays in our lives. What is striking about their answers is that, so often, rather than telling me what they think, people instead talk about how social media makes them *feel*. For many of us, social media has become intimately connected with our emotional selves. These types of conversations often lead me to conclude that what the internet runs on is not LOL cats or conspiracy theories or toddlers biting each other's fingers but something much simpler and more profound: emotion. Post a selfie that gets a lot of likes? You'll feel good, buzzing even. Post a selfie that gets digital tumbleweeds? The rancid prick of self-loathing will surely follow. By performing our lives online, we open ourselves up to a rollercoaster of emotions, with enough highs, lows and twists every week to make a soap opera seem sedate by comparison. If this sounds exhausting, that's because it can be. It's also contagious.

Given how emotions drive our attention, it's no surprise that social media companies would want to understand more deeply the relationship between their platforms and users' feelings. This interest led to a now notorious mass experiment. In 2012 Facebook, with the help of Cornell University, decided to research a phenomenon known as 'emotional contagion'.[9] If that sounds a little disease-y, it's because emotional contagion functions somewhat like a virus whereby one person's emotional state produces the same state or similar in others by virtue of proximity. The aim of the experiment was straightforward: Facebook wanted to explore how emotional contagion functions on its platform. What they discovered was startling. Over the course of a week, without the users concerned knowing they were part of a massive experiment, Facebook altered the newsfeed of a random sample of some 689,003 accounts. One group had their feeds altered to remove negative news, the other positive news. Then, researchers monitored if these positive and negative newsfeeds impacted the kinds of status updates users produced. Perhaps unsurprisingly, they found that those with negative feeds were more likely to produce negative status updates, and vice versa. While this doesn't capture what users felt per se, it does suggest that on social media what we see bears at least some connection to what we share, which may in turn link to how we feel. Fundamentally, it suggests that what we are exposed to on social media – depending on our susceptibility – shapes our reactions.

Facebook's experiment raises a couple of important points, one of which is the issue of informed consent (which was not sought from the tens of thousands of users in question, a fact that caused much subsequent outcry) and the other, the complex interplay between emotion and technology. Both points are rooted in the larger issue of how the data that accrues when we engage online is used – and abused. It is worth noting that in a subsequent study exploring emotional contagion on Twitter, researchers made a distinction between users who were highly susceptible to emotional contagion and those who were not.[10] While we certainly need more research in this area, if you are concerned about the impact of social media on your emotional health, it is worth stopping to consider which of these two camps you may fall into on any given day. 'Catching' someone else's positive emotions via social media on a bad day could be a way to lift the spirits – or it can serve to rub your face in whatever is making you feel blue. If you suspect that a high susceptibility for emotional contagion is making social media feel like a drag, those are entirely legitimate grounds to question if these technologies are enriching your life or depleting it. Paying attention to how our use of these platforms shapes our mood is one step to getting a clearer idea of how best to engage with them, if at all.

Cultivating a critical awareness of social media as an inherently ambivalent space is important because it helps us better understand the risks, pleasures and vulnerabilities that come with being visible on these platforms. Rather than feeling like frauds about the self we create online, we should remind ourselves that these spaces and activities are primed for contradiction. When appearing in public to an audience that is known and unknown to us, where the potential for judgement and a lack of control over our image is ever present, it is hardly surprising that we go about this strategically. This inevitably puts us in tension with expectations that we be 'real' and 'authentic', forgetting that the media, by its nature, is *mediated*; it is an intermediary between what *is* and our attempts to represent it. Representations, as any good scholar of media and culture will tell you, are an attempt to represent reality. They are not the real thing. This distinction is important to hold on to when trying to flatten ourselves to fit within the confines of what social media allows and rewards. It is also something to keep in mind when the urge to judge strikes, for all of us are more complex and more human than our avatars allow for.

Retaining a sense of our own humanity and that of others can help to navigate the emotional minefield that social media represents both online and offline. This may seem like a strange statement to make: after all, social media *is* an online phenomenon, but how we as individuals interact with these platforms has as much to do with who we are and how we feel offline as it does online.

Take FOMO, otherwise known as 'fear of missing out', often because viewing content online makes you assume others are having a great time while you, sadly, are not. Researchers found that those most likely to suffer from FOMO are often dissatisfied with their lives, which leads them to feel isolated, lacking in autonomy and ability.[11] This lack isn't caused by social media but it can be exacerbated by it and this may in turn lead us to rely more heavily on social media than we would if we were more content in general.

In his book *The Twittering Machine*, Richard Seymour cautions that our susceptibility to become hooked on the platform begins long before we log in.[12] Social media can help take the edge off the loneliness and boredom but it can also spark a cycle of reliance that has the potential to be, if not destructive, then a colossal time sink. This sink distracts us from the real and often difficult but necessary work we could be doing to build a more meaningful life and better connections with the people in it. As Seymour writes, 'we prefer the machine when human relationships have become disappointing'.[13] This risks turning us into what psychotherapist Nathaniel Branden called 'approval addicts' who rely on other people to determine their sense of self-worth, a path that can only lead to unhappiness.[14] Social media is designed to exploit these vulnerabilities, hoovering up our attention while distracting us from our goals. We may not pay for these distraction machines in monetary terms but we do pay in ways that are no less important: with our time and our emotions, which could be better spent pursuing more fulfilling activities. As tech ethics philosopher James Williams argues, when it comes to social media, 'We pay attention with the lives we might have lived.'[15]

A central issue here is avoidance. Social media provides a handy distraction from the sticky parts of our lives we would rather not think about. Distractions can be welcome and even necessary sometimes. But if we become perpetually distracted by technologies designed to prey on humanity's cognitive weaknesses, our minds consumed by the machine rather than material reality, we are not able to face up to what we must if we seek to be balanced individuals whose sense of self is not unduly reliant on external stimuli and validation.

A dark but highly entertaining exploration of this is the 2017 film *Ingrid Goes West.*[16] Starring Aubrey Plaza as alone-in-the-world Ingrid and Elisabeth Olsen as Californian Instagram influencer Taylor, the film follows Ingrid's ill-advised and eventually unhinged attempt to wrangle her way into Taylor's West Coast life. Ingrid is lonely, suffering from the loss of her mother and a subsequent stint in a psychiatric facility. Her life revolves around her phone and especially Instagram, which becomes a substitute for the connection she craves in every aspect of her life. As the film charts Ingrid's descent into mania while also skewering Taylor's Insta-perfect image, it captures the emptiness in both their lives. What gives the satire its emotional heft is that Ingrid is given chances to make meaningful connections and to be accepted for who she is rather than what she longs to be but she fails to take them, preferring instead to chase a fantasy. Heartbroken and alone, Ingrid looks for solutions and love in all the wrong places. In the hall of mirrors that is social media, she can see everything except herself.

Becoming aware of how we navigate visibility on social media, including taking steps to reclaim control over our minds and emotions and protect our privacy, not to mention time, is a positive. However, individualised approaches to the demands of online visibility have their limits. This is especially true when it comes to phenomena such as image-based abuse, which exploits the surveillance and circulation capacity of social media and the lack of control people have over their content. This lack of control is rooted in a technological infrastructure where the publishing and dissemination of sensitive material has never been easier, with perpetrators often facing little in the way of punishment. As the previous chapter outlined, this reality requires shifts at a cultural, legal and governmental level.

Yet the pace of change thus far has been so slow it leaves many victims of these types of offences feeling isolated and terrified at a time when they desperately need support. Developing harassment laws fit for the digital age, for example, can feel like playing a long game of catch-up. Before #MeToo erupted around the world, image-based abuse was already rife. In the US, for example, it took until the mid-2010s for lawmakers and platforms such as Reddit, spurred on by the fallout from the Fappening, to meaningfully begin to develop approaches to tackle it. In her book *Nobody's Victim*,[17] US attorney and innovator in sexual privacy law Carrie Goldberg, who has herself experienced the threat of image-based abuse, urges women not to willingly accept victimhood. Evoking the spirit of the collective, her approach advocates that women support one another using the law. She argues that some of the biggest obstacles faced by women affected by these crimes is a sense that they are on their own and therefore unable to seek justice; that they are somehow to blame for what has happened, and what has happened isn't a big deal because it took place online. All of this misses the fact that, as Goldberg writes, whether the attack happens online or offline, 'it's *all* real life [emphasis Goldberg's].'[18] This situation is compounded by advice like 'block and delete', which is not sufficient to match the craven and often sophisticated ways abusers use digital technologies to toy with their victims. Add to this the inaction of social media companies, many of whom, until quite recently, have been far too slow to tackle the abuse on their platforms.

Meanwhile, on a cultural level, old-fashioned judgements about female sexuality cloud the reality of what these crimes represent – namely the violation of a woman's right to privacy and bodily autonomy. As Goldberg and many others argue, this is about consent, a concept rooted in respect for the dignity of all human beings. But in the world of Silicon Valley where 'move fast and break things'[19] is a guiding maxim, vulnerability and questions of human dignity have, until quite recently, barely got a look in. Technology's gender gap and lack of diversity impacts not only the design of platforms but their outlook too. This lack of what Seyi Akiwowo described to me as an 'intersectional lens' or an awareness of different user needs risks further marginalising those already on the margins. Simply put, in a male-dominated environment, issues such as gender-based harassment are not going to be high on the agenda because those in power are far less likely to be affected by them. This is reflected not only in the priorities of tech companies but in society itself, where cultural attitudes still lag when it comes to understanding the impact of digital abuse.

Addressing this lag requires new tools and new language to help articulate the specificity of these harms. Taking 'image-based sexual abuse' or IBSA as an example, this terminology not only underpins legal mechanisms that deter and punish perpetrators, it challenges the misleading idea of revenge porn on a cultural level. Although beloved by the press, revenge porn as a term is an inaccurate representation of the harms committed against victims of these crimes.

Firstly, the notion of 'porn' can confer the idea that consent has been secured when the reality could not be further from the truth. Secondly, it also suggests the notion of entertainment or spectacle, as if looking at these images and videos is merely naughty rather than a violation, one designed to destroy another human being's life.

Writing in the *Oxford Journal of Legal Studies*, Clare McGlynn and Erika Rackley, the law professors who coined the term 'image-based sexual abuse', argue that revenge porn belongs to a group of popular terms that minimise the harms they describe, such as 'up skirting' (which was made illegal in England in 2019), or in the case of events, the Fappening.[20] These jokey terms also obfuscate the interconnectedness of these online phenomena, arising as they do from the intersection of age-old misogynistic attitudes with the capabilities of digital technology. As McGlynn and Rackley emphasise, these harms do not happen in isolation; they reflect and exist on a long continuum of violence against women, aspects of which have become emboldened by new technologies. Salacious wording such as revenge porn erases the awfulness of what these terms refer to, namely gender-based harassment and abuse. Neither do such terms capture the fuller picture, that is, how these activities form part of an overarching misogynistic online culture requiring a coherent, robust response from the law.

Simply put, language matters. 'Image-based sexual abuse' emphasises these activities for what they are: a form of sexual abuse and a crime. Since I first wrote about revenge porn in Ireland in the mid-2010s, how the press covers the issue has thankfully changed somewhat. Granted, there are still too many unfortunate headlines using the term; but increasingly, revenge porn is being redefined more accurately as image-based sexual abuse. In helping to change the law, McGlynn and Rackley also gifted the wider culture a definition that encapsulates the serious nature of these activities, most especially the fact that they are *crimes*, and no less significant than their offline counterparts. This definition does something that Goldberg also emphasises in her work: it centres the victim and the harm done to them, alongside the necessity for justice. In doing so, it shifts common understandings towards seeing these activities for the harm they cause and their victims as deserving of compassion and support instead of blame.

Corresponding with Professor McGlynn over email in October 2020, she says, 'We have seen a rise in all forms of online abuse as a result of the Covid pandemic, including all forms of image-based sexual abuse. It is more important than ever that we recognise the nature of the harms of these forms of abuse and enable victim-survivors to take action.' She goes on to describe what victim-survivors of these crimes experience as a type of 'social rupture': 'their lives become separated into a "before" and "after" the abuse. They experience an all-encompassing breach of trust. They also experience harms of isolation, where they are cut off from friends, family and society more broadly as they withdraw from social media.'

'Online abuse not only amplifies the harms but also changes the way that abuse is perpetrated,' she writes. 'Laws which clearly tackle these forms of abuse can let victims know that their experiences and harms are understood; we recognise that they have been harmed; and they send a message that society treats these abuses as wrong.'

In the last chapter I mentioned the work of Associate Professor Emma A. Jane who is based at the University of New South

Wales. Her book *Misogyny Online: A Short (and Brutish) History*[21] explores the rise of gendered hate in the digital age. Over email, I ask Jane about the role cultural attitudes play in people's misperceptions of the harms caused by online abuse, especially the assumption that online abuse is somehow less damaging than its offline counterpart. She points out that, whatever the context, there is no one or 'right way' to experience abuse so we need to keep in mind 'the wide variation in individual response and the importance of considering context, intersectional issues, and so on'.

Describing the distinction between the offline and online worlds as a 'pernicious myth', she outlines how real the effects of online abuse can be for those on the receiving end of it, describing the impact on victims she has spoken to in the past:

> Harms in the supposedly 'virtual' world can have real, bodily and physical effects, as per accounts given by the gendered cyberhate targets I've interviewed who describe their experiences online in somatic terms. They report, for instance, that being attacked feels like 'being kicked in the guts', 'slapped in the face' and 'vomited on', as well as reporting physical manifestations such as increased heartbeat, sweating, nausea, feeling the hair on the back of their neck stand on end, experiencing cold chills, and so on. In other words, seemingly disembodied discourse online can have a significant embodied impact that manifests in bodies.

Jane points out what many users know to be true: that the internet has long since evolved beyond being an optional space that we can simply vacate when things get tough. It has become enmeshed in every aspect of daily life, from banking to grocery shopping to socialising to work:

> It is important that harms such as cyberbullying, cyberhate, and cyber abuse are recognised as significant not just because of the flow-on impacts on the physical domain, but because the virtual world is now an *inherently* significant part of contemporary life. When police advise gendered cyberhate victims to 'take a little break' from using the internet, it is on par with suggesting they stay locked down in their homes rather than risk venturing outdoors.

I ask why she thinks the internet has become such a fertile place for misogyny and Jane links back to the prevailing equalities that shape modern societies, raising once again the role of culture:

> The fact that so many men are using the affordances offered by the internet to abuse so many women using the rhetoric of gendered violence is both diagnostic and constitutive of the fact that men continue to hold a disproportionate share of political, economic and social power, and use various forms of violence against women to maintain the inequitable status quo. In a nutshell, the internet is a fertile ground for misogyny first and foremost because – despite decades of concerted feminism – sexism, misogyny and androcentrism remain grossly prevalent in the broader culture. Similarly, this also explains why the internet is also such a fertile ground for racism, homophobia, transphobia, able-ism, and so on.

When I ask Jane for three things she would change about the internet to make it less of a hive for misogyny, the first thing she mentions is governmental inaction when it comes to holding social media companies accountable, especially in relation to harms against the individual and against democracy. Citing the role of social media in the rise of misinformation and disinformation along with human rights abuses in Myanmar, the Philippines and elsewhere and diminishing human well-being in general, she, like Jaron Lanier, wants to see more people delete their accounts:

> Deleting all or most of one's social media accounts (as I and increasing numbers of concerned people have done) is not just a simple economic boycott. Given that the product here is not the app itself but rather the accumulation of small modifications in mass behaviour – in *our* behaviour – the power of this boycott is that we are depriving these exploitative and manipulative corporations not of their customers (which are those shifty entities who pay for access to users' data) but *of their most critical raw component.*
>
> If enough people delete their social media accounts, it will be like depriving a baker of flour. It will force big tech to find other business models and perhaps even pave the way for non-profit social media platforms, or perhaps social media platforms in which the exchange is clear (for example, I pay a subscription, and you offer me a product without any of the sleazy privacy invasion or behaviour manipulation and modification).

Her final wish is a simple one that, if ever realised, could transform much more than just social media:

> I wish I had the ability to instil in all humans a deep respect for difference, a warm curiosity about the experience of others, and greater kindness, compassion, and empathy. In my experiences, most disputes are nothing more than ALL-CAPS SCREAMING MATCHES more likely to further cement interlocuters' existing views that open spaces for greater understanding and empathy.

Preventing online harassment and building safe, accessible digital spaces is a both a local issue and a global one. Technology knows no borders, nor does inequality. Founded in 2012, the Digital Rights Foundation (DRF) is an NGO based in Pakistan that advocates for human rights, democratic processes and digital governance. Although it focuses on women's right to access digital spaces and tackling online harassment, the DRF's wider vision is one where everyone in the world can exercise their right to expression through free internet access along with robust privacy protections. DRF's founder, lawyer and activist Nighat Dad, now sits on Facebook's Oversight Board,[22] which was established in 2020. The board's forty members are charged with helping to decide what content Facebook and Instagram should permit or remove, informed by their expertise and a respect for freedom of expression and human rights.

Messaging Dad about the important work the DRF does, I ask for her thoughts on the distinction between offline and online harassment. 'Attitudes like this are extremely dangerous in a society like Pakistan, where perpetrators of violence are often left off the hook,' she writes back:

> This attitude stems from an underappreciation for the strong effects of mental health on an individual. Physical violence has two aspects to it, the physical pain and mental trauma. Online violence is not 'physical' – however, it is mental trauma. The attitude of disregarding online violence as unimportant is indicative of our general attitude towards mental health and the trauma related to it.

Dad's motivation for setting up DRF stemmed from a weariness of working in 'the male-dominated world of law' and a desire to be a change-maker for her community:

> I saw that digital rights and law would be the future, and that few people were working on legislation and advocacy in the country. I started DRF in 2012, and since then I have assembled a team of strong women who are equally passionate about digital rights in the country. DRF is working to achieve fair and equal internet access for everyone and is also working on creating safe online spaces for women and gender minorities since these communities face the most online harassment and violence.

When I ask about the harm inaction on gender-based online harassment causes, Dad highlights how it compounds the sense of exclusion marginalised people already feel, contributing to the digital divide phenomenon:

> Inaction leads to more online violence and harassment, and thus, women and gender minorities

> feel that online space, like all other spaces, is not for them and they retreat from using it. They are deprived of using online spaces and technologies, and thus are not able to take advantage of the many opportunities that new technologies give all of us on a daily basis.

Creating change, Dad says, means being organised and proactive in demanding that both governments and social media companies take action:

> The major way to remedy this is to take part in active advocacy against these structures and to hold social media companies accountable for their decisions and their inaction on these issues. Stakeholder groups need to act together against these actions not only by social media companies, but also by legislators who have globally been late to pass law that ensures internet and data safety and privacy. The responsibility for this issue does not solely lay on social media companies, but also governments who need to legislate for online spaces so that a majority of a population may benefit from it.

As we've seen so far, while social media companies are quick to sell visibility as a key appeal of their products, they are less quick to act when that visibility goes awry. Online abuse is a classic example, where cries of 'protect free speech' reflect the ethos of the technology's creators at the expense of those subjected to forms of speech that are unacceptable and sometimes even illegal in the offline world, as in the case of hate speech. How to address the need for change on these platforms and how best to get companies to take greater responsibility for the consequences of their products are issues researchers and activists across the world are grappling with today. Many of these issues stem from a point that bears repeating: these platforms have evolved so quickly, absorbing more and more of our lives while creating new vulnerabilities, that governments and the law are on the back foot, forced to play catch-up. Another factor that makes setting standards and regulations difficult is the globalised nature of social media and, more broadly, digital technology. This represents a real challenge for campaigners: how can we create robust rules for companies whose activities take place in hundreds of different geographical areas, all of which have their own laws and cultures? One idea is to take inspiration from a widely used legal framework with global respect and recognition, one used by the DRF, Amnesty International and many other organisations; one that centres human dignity: international human rights.

'The digital revolution is a major global human rights issue. Its unquestionable benefits do not cancel out its unmistakable risks.'[23] In October 2019 Michelle Bachelet, High Commissioner for Human Rights, delivered a speech in New York on human rights in the digital age. Acknowledging the huge potential of these technologies, Bachelet also drew attention to the threat they pose to the individual and to democratic freedom: '[We can't] afford to see cyberspace and artificial intelligence as an ungoverned or ungovernable space – a human rights black hole. The same rights exist online and offline.'[24] A few months before Bachelet delivered her speech, David Kaye, Michel Forst and Clément Voule, UN Special Rapporteurs on freedom of opinion and expression, issued a similar warning, telling an audience in Geneva, 'Digital space is not a neutral space. At the levels of its physical architecture, regulation and use, different groups exert their interests over it. The principles of international human rights law, however, should be at the centre of its development.'[25]

A year before in 2018, in response to the growing threat of digital abuse, the UN Human Rights Council adopted a resolution to accelerate efforts 'to eliminate violence against women and girls: preventing and responding to violence against women and girls in digital contexts'.[26] The resolution also called on 'businesses to implement the Guiding Principles on Business and Human Rights, protect the private data of women and girls, create transparent and effective processes for reporting violence, and develop policies that meaningfully protect women and girls from violence in digital contexts'.[27] Echoing the Council, a 2018 paper in the journal *Policy & Internet*[28] by a group of Australia-based academics makes a persuasive case for the effectiveness of using these guiding principles[29] to tackle gender-based online abuse.

Although not legally binding, the UN's Guiding Principles on Business and Human Rights are the most authoritative international statement in existence relating to companies' human-rights responsibilities. These principles are derived from the United Nations' core document: *The Universal Declaration of Human Rights*, which enshrines the rights and freedoms of all human beings. The principles require companies to acknowledge that they, just like governments, have human-rights responsibilities.

The authors of the paper argue that close adherence to these principles would help compel technology companies, including social media giants, to strengthen their oversight in key areas. They also propose that three of these could be acted on immediately. Firstly, 'enhanced transparency': companies would be expected to be more open about how their products impact on human rights and what the authors term their 'internal governance practices', which could potentially shed greater light on how issues such as shadow banning, moderation techniques and algorithmic biases affect users. Next, commit to ensuring that the 'design and deployment' of their products is conducted with human rights in mind. This could mean, for example, that dating-app designers consciously consider the reality of sexual harassment by building in features to keep users safe *prior* to their release into the market. By committing to exercising due diligence at the level of design and policy, companies would also acknowledge that they have a level of responsibility when it comes to developing solutions to human-rights violations that may occur on their platforms. Lastly, social media companies would be expected to 'develop and apply clear, consistent processes' to deal with abuse, rather than current approaches, which can be slow and patchy in their application.

While this all sounds promising, the authors caution that securing the commitment of technology companies will require the combined efforts of diverse stakeholders, among them civil society and activists, but governments have a particular role to pay. This chimes with earlier points made by Jane and Dad. Without strong laws, there is little to require companies to act, aside from social pressure. This can be effective (as with the *New York Times* report on Pornhub's many failings) but is never guaranteed. It is also an unlikely long-term solution as it doesn't 'cement' in place processes or standards or create an independent body powerful enough to hold companies legally accountable. Sure, it might be a good PR look for a social media company to trumpet its commitment to the Guiding Principles on Business and Human Rights and some good may come out of that trumpeting. But performing a hat-tip towards important but non-legally binding standards versus being forced to act consistently and meaningfully in keeping with those standards because you are legally obliged to present two different prospects.

Under a human-rights framework, companies would also have to re-evaluate how to balance the protection of free speech that is so much a part of their own DNA (as they are not considered publishers by law, social media companies are not subjected to the same rules as traditional media in this regard) with their obligation to tackle hate speech, incitement to violence and discrimination. This is undoubtedly a complex issue and one that needs to be carefully calibrated to respect the vital role free speech plays in democratic processes. But women's ability to express themselves online should not be infringed upon by those using 'freedom of speech' to make threats of gender-based violence and intimidation, including racism, homophobia and other forms of prejudice, with an impunity that would never be tolerated in the offline world. Striking this balance is set to be an ongoing process rather than a fixed one, but these complexities must be faced sooner rather than later if we are to build inclusive, accessible digital spaces for all.

The visibility trap works most powerfully when it weaves together long-standing sexist attitudes with the capabilities of digital technology to discipline and target women. But these attitudes are not only external to the technology; often, they are built into it. Bringing a human-rights perspective to the design of social media would revise the idea that this technology is inherently neutral or objective. This assumption of neutrality blinds engineers to how design can intensify and reproduce sexism, racism and other inequalities. It is also reflective of the lack of diversity in the industry, where the absence of different viewpoints around the design table contributes to a myopia on the complex ways people experience the world. This means that creators are not required to meet the challenges this reality presents, although doing so could produce innovative and effective design measures that would make for much safer, better-to-use products. Tinder, for example, recently introduced new features to combat harassment on the app.[30] While this is welcome, if overdue, Tinder users are still left with a blocking system that deletes the conversation in question, meaning there is no record of it. For those wanting to pursue their harasser through the justice system, this could be crucial evidence, which could be easily preserved if the app were designed differently.[31]

Failure to meaningfully tackle online abuse through the kind of coherent framework offered by human-rights law runs the risk that this behaviour becomes normalised through persistence. To abusers it says, don't worry – you can say what you want, post what you want, ruin whoever's life, because around here, the rules are that there are no rules. Without boundaries (such as those that exist, broadly speaking, in public life), this antisocial behaviour can escalate with no fear of repercussion, except for those on the receiving end of it, on sites that unironically describe themselves as 'social'. Other than governments, no one is more powerfully equipped to change their platforms than social media companies themselves. Experts and activists around the world have lots of inspired ideas for how they might do so: taking a human-rights approach is one of them.

Change, by definition, is rarely easy. This is especially true when you are living through a rapidly evolving technological revolution the likes of which humanity hasn't seen since the Gutenberg printing press cranked up in the fifteenth century. To be alive in the twenty-first century is to be a guinea pig in an economic and cultural shift that is profoundly changing how humans relate to one another, the impacts of which we will only understand in retrospect. But the work of countering the negatives of this change can't wait for history to make its pronouncements: out of necessity, it has started already. For the individual, this includes developing a critical awareness about the place of social media in our lives, asking what precisely we are using it for and what we are receiving in return. Deleting your accounts as Jaron Lanier and others urge may be an option. Figuring out our boundaries and being selective about what we consume and expose ourselves to online can help users negotiate a level of visibility with which they feel comfortable, as can protecting our content and being security conscious at all times. This is not a perfect solution. It requires willpower and the ability to log off without facing financial consequences or increased isolation.

But if you can create the space to reset your relationship to social media, it may enable you to evaluate the factors influencing how you use these platforms and gain deeper insight into yourself in the process. Your decreased attention also hits social companies where it hurts: their bottom line. If enough people felt compelled to dramatically reduce their use of platforms as they are, it could motivate companies to reimagine their offerings or inspire competitors to produce new ones that don't rely on surveillance or exploiting vulnerabilities in human psychology for profit.

In March 2021 I received a press release from the digital rights organisation Access Now[32] with the headline: 'After nearly two decades in the dark, Facebook releases its human rights policy.' 'We are committed to respecting human rights as set out in the United Nations Guiding Principles on Business and Human Rights,' Facebook's long-awaited statement[33] read, mentioning human rights due diligence and disclosure, promising to adhere to human rights policies, including providing access to remedy and maintaining oversight, governance, and accountability. It also stated that 'we commit to strong diversity and inclusion practises in our workplace as one important driver of equality in our workplace, and as a vital input for the development of products and policies that bring equal value to all people'.

Thanks in no small part to the tireless work of activists and advocates and growing public concern, over the last few years some social media companies have become more proactive when it comes to tackling abuse on their platforms. Facebook's human rights announcement is the latest of a number of changes at the company. In 2019 it strengthened its approach to the non-consensual sharing of images by introducing machine-learning and AI programs designed to spot such content and remove it, without the need for the victim to lodge a report.[34] It also introduced photo-match technology to stop the sharing of non-consensual images and an online resource hub to support victims in reporting these abuses.[35] These important changes came about after the company began working with victim-advocate organisations such as the Cyber Civil Rights Initiative and the DRF.[36] Although more remains to be done to curb the distribution of non-consensual images and other forms of abuse, these changes indicate a welcome willingness on Facebook/Instagram's behalf to engage with stakeholders and victims, which in turn sends a message to users and the wider culture about the serious and harmful nature of these activities. While social media companies are not the only part of the equation when it comes to tackling image-based online abuse, they are a core element. The examples they set, the antisocial behaviour they tolerate or refuse to tolerate and the rules they enforce matter, especially for those on the margins.

Instagram, meanwhile, has also been responding to criticism of a different kind that is specific to the cultures it fosters, centring around censorship (as discussed in Chapter Three), the impact of its competitive comparison culture on users' self-esteem and body image and the peddling of dubious diet-culture products.[37] In some jurisdictions the company has been experimenting with making likes invisible except to the person on the receiving end of them, a process known as 'demetrication'. This involves lowering the visibility of numerical ranking mechanisms such as likes and shares on social media platforms to help reduce compulsive behaviours and feelings of inadequacy.[38] In these trials, individuals can see the likes on their posts but their followers cannot. While this may go some way to reducing judgement and the pressure to produce 'perfect' images (something we will require proper research to establish), it still ties users to a never-ending popularity contest, even if it is for their eyes only.

When we reduce ourselves to metrics and outsource our self-esteem to others, not having them see our 'mark' or 'result' may diminish feelings of shame, but it doesn't address the root issue, which lies in how these technologies exploit our desire for validation and for visibility in the first place. Similarly, Instagram's recent moves to restrict exposure for those under the age of eighteen to influencer marketing that makes 'a miraculous claim' regarding diet products or cosmetic surgery is welcome[39] – but it doesn't address the harms done to those over-eighteens or the harms caused by the pervasiveness of these cultures online. Neither does it address how accurate (or not) these companies' verification systems are when it comes to determining who is and isn't of age. Nor does it disincentivise this kind of marketing or the body-centric focus it fosters, which is rampant in certain sections of influencer culture. If the aim is to reduce the pressure to be perfect then a good place to start would be to engage with those who use the platform to push unattainable, unhealthy models of beauty and those who look up to them with a view to developing a more ethical and transparent content framework. The move towards clearly declaring sponsored posts and #ads is a step in the right direction but much more remains to be done.

Making online visibility less of a trap requires a multilayered approach, incorporating the personal, the political, the cultural and the technological. As these platforms become ever more enmeshed with our lives, developing processes to help stop or remedy their worst excesses is one aspect to consider. Another is reimagining how platforms could look if they weren't driven by profit models that treat all engagement, no matter how bullying or undemocratic, as a metric from which to extract value. This is not about chasing some utopia: it is about corporate accountability, creator responsibility and developing oversight processes fit for the challenges of the modern world that uphold the common good. For women, accessing social media should not have to mean tolerating abuse that would never be acceptable in offline contexts. Nor should it mean diminished self-esteem or the fear of social or professional invisibility if they cannot fit into the parameters set by these platforms.

For over ten years now, social media companies have been given free rein to impress us with the promise of visibility and new ways to connect. From here, the benefits and ill-effects of that promise need to be more closely interrogated rather than accepted: because without the necessary protections, greater digital media literacy and a serious shift in our cultural mindset, visibility will remain a trap.

Afterword

In May 2020 a New York judge ruled that Lauren Miranda could move forward with her unfair dismissal suit against the school district that formerly employed her. Afterwards, her lawyer commended the court's decision, framing it as a step forward for equality. 'In the past, the previous generation perceived exposed breasts as prurient, sexual, carnal,' he told the press. 'The millennials don't see it that way.'[1] For Miranda, the decision validated her desire for justice while also sending a clear message about fighting back against sexist double standards. She told reporters, 'I'm standing up for myself and for other women – showing my students that when someone does something wrong, you need to stand up for yourself, even if it's a tough fight.'[2]

While Miranda is yet to have her day in court, her refusal to be silenced or to accept having her career destroyed because of a selfie represents one of the first cases of its kind but it is unlikely to be the last. While there is a growing awareness of the harms of non-consensual image-sharing, victim-blaming and a distrust of female sexuality persist on social media platforms as much as they have done offline for centuries. As Miranda's case shows – and so many others' throughout this book – those challenging these ideas tend to be women who have found themselves at the receiving end. Rather than retreating, they are willing – often at great personal cost – to put their stories into the public domain to open people's eyes to how powerfully regressive ideas about gender find expression online. This work is ongoing and urgent, and these women driving it are heroes.

Just as I finished drafting this book and weeks before Ireland's image-based abuse laws were finally approved by the government, a huge database was discovered, created by 500 individuals and containing thousands of intimate images of Irish women.[3] Some of the pictures came from sites such as Instagram while others had been taken when victims were unaware they were being photographed. Megan Sims, one of the activists who brought the existence of the database to public attention, told me: 'There is no respect for women as people. Their photos are traded – if someone perceives another girl to be better looking, your photos will be traded for hers like Pokémon cards. Women are still seen as objects.'

After a police investigation, no evidence of criminal harmdoing was found.[4] Around the same time as this issue was playing out in Ireland, the online publication *Motherboard* reported that non-consensual pornographic images and videos taken from notorious websites were being used as part of a database to create 'machine learning-generated porn'. A victim whose abusive video might someday be used in this way told *Motherboard* of her hope the footage of her assault might never resurface, adding, 'but there is always someone who manages to fish it out from the depths of the internet'.[5]

Miranda's case, whenever it is heard, will take place in a world where digital technology and social media plays an even greater part in everyday life. This shift was already well underway before the pandemic but the events of 2020–21 have greatly accelerated its effects. While this has its positives in terms of remote working, keeping in touch with our loved ones during lockdown etc., it also produced effects that are a bleak indicator of how technology is reinforcing inequality. One issue is the sharp rise in image-based abuse in Europe and elsewhere during lockdowns, but this is only part of the picture.

In October 2020 a Plan International survey of 14,000 girls across multiple continents found that in both high- and low-income countries, girls using social media are 'routinely subjected to explicit messages, pornographic photos, cyberstalking and other distressing forms of abuse, and reporting tools are ineffective in stopping it'.[6] Respondents told Plan International how this affects them emotionally, causing fear, stress, anxiety, poor body image and a reluctance to use social media, even though they had come to rely on it more than ever during lockdowns. Where once catcalling and lewd remarks were something that occurred in public, for many of the girls Plan International spoke to, social media brought this harassment into their private spaces to the extent that 50 per cent of respondents said online harassment is more common than street harassment. Meanwhile, in November 2020 the UN Committee for the Elimination of Discrimination Against Women (CEDAW) called for social media companies to do more to stop platforms being used as a channel for human trafficking in the context of rising online demand during the pandemic. In a statement CEDAW urged social media companies to 'set up relevant controls to mitigate the risk of exposing women and girls to trafficking and sexual exploitation' and to use the data they collate 'to identify traffickers and involved parties from the demand side'.[7]

Speaking to *Vogue* in the same month, celebrated French-Moroccan novelist Leïla Slimani discussed her decision to quit social media.[8] In an industry where being active on the likes of Twitter and Instagram is now regarded as an integral part of one's job as a writer or journalist, her decision to not just step back from these spaces but to disappear from them entirely might be seen as ill-advised. But rather than it supporting her creative work, Slimani found social media stifling. Evoking the Victorian notion of 'the angel in the house' domestic archetype (who Virginia Woolf believed women writers needed to kill to be free to do their work),[9] she spoke of the need to kill 'the angel' on Instagram and to reject the necessity for external validation to protect her ability to think and write freely.

She also acknowledged the positives: how social media had enabled her activism, connecting her to women around the world and making lots of new friends. But the downsides, like lack of accountability, which she saw as leading to a 'reign of impunity and demagoguery', outweighed the good.[10] When asked whether she was worried about losing out professionally by not being so present online, she replied, 'They want to think that it's an obligation to be on social media, and I'm not sure that's true. But if it is true, that doesn't mean that we don't need to change certain things about it.'[11]

Users negotiate with online visibility every day, deciding what to share, how to be seen and what to consume. Thanks to the advancement of digital technologies, we live as never before in a world of images, each one embodying, as John Berger famously wrote, a way of seeing.[12] This way of seeing extends beyond the image itself to the cultural and economic factors governing its production, a point that remains as true of images today as it ever was, with one additional but no less important element: the image's reception and circulation on social media platforms and all the baggage that comes with it. By turning ourselves into representations for judgemental audiences, we risk existing less for ourselves than for others.

This dissonance grows louder and louder the more we invest in those known and unknown to us, letting them determine our sense of reality and our sense of self. We love and hate our selfies because they are idealised versions of ourselves we know we can never fully become – although we might want to, sometimes desperately. Technology such as beauty apps show us what we could be while emphasising what we are not, enabling us to send a fantasy self – one that both delights and shames us – out to meet the critical gaze of the digital world. We do not set the terms of this visibility; social media and society do, but we conform to it nevertheless because not to feels like risking invisibility, an even harsher denial of the self.

Social media, we are told, is much more democratic than older forms of media such as television and radio – on here, anyone can be seen. *There are no stuffy gatekeepers in this new land, kids. Just download the app and get snapping/tweeting/swiping!* And while it is true that anyone with an internet-enabled phone can broadcast themselves using these platforms, the question of being seen and indeed heard is no less elitist and hierarchical on social media than it is on its precursors. The censorship of unruly feminine bodies and communities that sit outside the norm, for example, indicate that just because mechanisms such as algorithms are 'technological', they are no less inclined towards ideological bias than any other form of editorial direction. Whereas a newspaper's bias might be easy to spot, the machinations of algorithms and moderation techniques remain shrouded in mystery despite governing what tens of millions of people across the world see – and don't see – online each day. Campaigners drawing attention to this lack of transparency, like Petra, Nyome and Rupi in Chapter Three, alert us all to how these platforms think about what deserves visibility, what doesn't, and how easily images – and by extension, all content – can be 'disappeared' by our corporate overloads.

Not everyone feels the lash of the algorithm, of course. KIC-style influencers enjoy a brand of visibility that is unlikely to be censured, no matter how close its proponents come to violating terms of service. But this does not mean that what it promotes is positive. It is a visibility that talks out of both sides of its mouth, calling in women while locking them out, dressed up to the nines to meet the male gaze, espousing 'empowerment' and sisterhood for a female gaze that veers towards the critical rather than the supportive. The KIC promises a roadmap to successful twenty-first-century womanhood, one that embraces visibility as a means to success and well-being at a time of economic, environmental and political meltdown, happily profiting from the pressures that arise from subjecting oneself to the unrelenting glare of a digital spotlight, the same pressures it celebrates and intensifies. As unattainable and edited as images of women in ads and magazines have ever been despite trying to appear more relatable and 'authentic', that this limited and limiting vision enjoys such a high degree of visibility on social media shows just how much 'new' technologies reflect and reproduce the same old stuff.

That same old stuff extends, sadly, to misogyny. Online visibility and the surveillance capacity of smartphones make women accessible, trackable and observable. From non-consensual image-sharing to digitally enabled intimate partner abuse to AI creating deepfake porn from filmed abuse, it means their images, and their privacy, can be endlessly exploited. When this occurs, responses are still too often informed by a failure to appreciate how damaging these violations are: they represent real harms and crimes, not simply an annoyance. All too often the onus is put on victims to avoid the internet, a further encroachment on their freedom while their abuser/s are able to carry on regardless. For choosing – and being encouraged to choose – visibility, women are rendered guilty for the attention they attract. Even as the world wakes up to how easily any of us could have our content exploited by bad actors, gender bias in the form of complicity and suspicion still inform reactions to women's experience of online abuse. Technology has advanced, breathing fresh life into misogyny, gifting it new weapons. But attitudes to harassment are still too often rooted in the past, haunted by the idea that if a woman is forced to wear a scold's bridle, well, then she must have done something to deserve it.

During that strange summer of 2020 I returned to a book I had read many years before, Mary Shelley's *Frankenstein*.[13] Written when Shelley was a teenager and published in 1818, it tells the tale of a brilliant young chemist named Victor Frankenstein who creates a human-like creature, known in popular culture as 'the Monster'. Although Victor initially had grand ambitions for his progeny, as the creature comes to life he is hit with disgust at what he has done, fleeing the scene, abandoning his creation to a lonely, desperate fate. Shelley's story draws on topical issues of the time, including the potential of new forms of science such as galvanism, which studied the interplay between electrical currents and biological material, raising the (highly unlikely) prospect of bringing the dead back to life. In building a being from discarded body parts and then animating it with electricity, Victor's ambitions certainly reflect those of his era but as Shelley shows, ambition without accountability is a dangerous thing.

In the two centuries since its publication, *Frankenstein* has become a shorthand and a framework for thinking about the intended and unintended consequences of scientific creation. As such, it is incessantly applicable, as I found when I settled down to write this book. For me, Shelley's novel is, at its heart, a cautionary tale about taking responsibility for the things human beings create and the horrors that ensue when we fail at this duty. Victor's creature only becomes a monster when his master and father rejects him, sparking a chain of events that will destroy many lives, including Victor's. This calamity might have been avoided if Victor had been motivated not as he was by ego, grief at his mother's death and unthinking passion, but by objectivity, a sense of personal and social responsibility and the wise counsel of other experts. Without humility and an ethical consciousness, a slave to dreams of exceptionalism, Victor realises that the act of creation can have dire unintended consequences only when it is too late.

It is not difficult to draw parallels between today's technological landscape and that of Shelley when the seeds of the industry as we know it now were first being planted. The questions of harm and responsibility she raised loom larger than ever. Despite what some critics argue, I don't think *Frankenstein* is a story about abandoning science or technology for something 'natural' and untainted by human endeavour. Instead, I see it as a warning and a challenge: what will we humans do with the tremendous responsibility the ability to create presents? Will we use it as Victor did, for personal gain at the expense of personal responsibility? Or will we work from an awareness of our fallibility as humans, building platforms and products that support the angels of our better nature rather than the devils of our worst? Can this be achieved with the internet landscape as it is, where profit is king, social accountability an afterthought and vast power is concentrated in the hands of a tiny few?

Social media companies have big questions to answer but as users navigating these spaces, so do we. These platforms have managed to weave their way into so many aspects of our lives that cutting them out in one fell swoop is not realistic, but reducing time spent on them and setting firm boundaries around how or if we use them certainly is; as is speaking up about their negative effects on our lives and on those we care about. So too is being mindful of what we put out into the digital ether, noting how what we engage with affects us and how we too contribute to toxic online cultures. Despite what the hashtags say, social media as it exists today is not built for kindness or productive discussions. It is built for judgement, for surveillance, for conflict, for emotional and behavioural manipulation. As users we should always be alert to how often platforms enable activities that are harmful for individuals and for society. Ask yourself: if a bar or café or clothing store did the same, would I keep frequenting them? Never lose sight of the fact that social media is a business, and good businesses look after their customers and uphold common decency.

The 'empowerment' social media sells women relies not on self-sufficiency or collective action or bold visions for a better future but on schoolgirl-level external validation, where how we feel about ourselves is determined not from the inside out but the outside in. You may get to be visible to a degree but the greatest levels of visibility are still reserved for those who look a certain way and are willing to perform an aesthetically appealing, commodified version of their life, with the time and resources to do so. This daily outsourcing of self-esteem risks letting metrics determine our worth, as if we were nothing more than another form of capital, ripe for exploitation. Women have fought for too long and too hard to be returned to object status by new technologies that talk the talk of equality without walking the walk. We can and should demand better: for ourselves, for each other, for our world and for those coming after us. Technology, like everything else created by humans, can be remade. Visibility needn't be a trap. Change is always possible. As Mary Shelley herself reportedly observed, the beginning is always today.[14]

Notes

Introduction

1. Liveline Interview, RTÉ Radio One. 23 June 2020. https://www.facebook.com/rteradio1/videos/roisin-sex-video-liveline/571465616896533.
2. Ibid.
3. Ibid.
4. Eva Wiseman. The Slane Girl Twitter scandal proves that women can't make mistakes. *The Guardian*, 1 September 2013. https://www.theguardian.com/lifeandstyle/2013/sep/01/slane-girl-twitter-scandal-women.
5. Lisa McInerney. Sharing of 'Slane Girl' pics does disservice to women and men. *The Journal*, 20 August 2013. https://www.thejournal.ie/readme/lisa-mcinerney-sharing-of-slane-girl-pics-does-disservice-to-both-women-and-men-1045153-Aug2013.
6. Wiseman, 2013.
7. Ibid.
8. RTÉ Radio One, 2020.
9. In February 2021 the Irish government passed the Harassment, Harmful Communications and Related Offences Bill. It was dubbed 'Coco's Law' after Nicole 'Coco' Fox Fenlon, who died by suicide aged 21 in 2018 after years of physical and online bullying.
10. Mary McGill. The Unkindest Cut: how sharing of intimate pictures can be devastating and dehumanising. *Sunday Business*

Post, 4 July 2020. https://www.businesspost.ie/life-arts/the-unkindest-cut-how-sharing-of-intimate-pictures-can-be-devastating-and-dehumanising-0be8d8a3.

11. David Lyon, *The Culture of Surveillance: Watching as a Way of Life* (Polity, 2018).
12. Online Abuse and Threats of Violence Against Female Politicians on the Rise. National University of Ireland, Galway, 2 October 2020. https://www.nuigalway.ie/about-us/news-and-events/news-archive/2020/october/online-abuse-and-threats-of-violence-against-female-politicians-on-the-rise.html.
13. Ibid.
14. Ibid.
15. Ibid.
16. Brian Kelly. Women sports stars more likely to get abuse on social media. *Galway Daily*, 3 October 2019. https://www.galwaydaily.com/news/women-sports-stars-more-likely-to-get-abuse-on-social-media.
17. Johnny Watterson. Bigots still creating cold reception for women in world of sports broadcasting. *The Irish Times*, 13 February 2021. https://www.irishtimes.com/sport/rugby/bigots-still-creating-a-cold-reception-for-women-in-world-of-sports-broadcasting-1.4483452.
18. Neil Treacy. It's just horrific, it's horrendous: Emer O'Neill on Tackling Online Abuse. *Newstalk*, 23 February 2021. https://www.newstalk.com/sport/its-just-horrific-its-horrendous-emer-oneill-on-tackling-online-abuse-1155018
19. John R. Culkin. A Schoolman's Guide to Marshall McLuhan. *The Saturday Review*, 18 March 1967. https://webspace.royalroads.ca/llefevre/wp-content/uploads/sites/258/2017/08/A-Schoolmans-Guide-to-Marshall-McLuhan-1.pdf.
20. Sarah Banet-Weiser, *Empowered: Popular Feminism and Popular Misogyny* (Duke University Press, 2018).
21. Jaron Lanier, *Ten Arguments for Deleting Your Social Media Accounts Right Now* (The Bodley Head, 2018).

One: Let's Get Visible

1. bell hooks, 'The Oppositional Gaze', *Black Looks: Race and Representation* (South End Press, 1992).
2. This Teacher Was Fired Over a Topless Photo. Now, She's Fighting Back. VICE News, 10 April 2019. https://www.youtube.com/watch?v=dhnIm76pz1M.
3. New York teacher who says she was fired 'lost everything' over topless selfie. 5 April 2019. https://abcnews.go.com/US/york-teacher-fired-lost-topless-selfie/story?id=62176028.
4. A Middle School Teacher Was Fired After A Student Obtained her Topless Selfie. Now She's Suing the School Board for Gender Discrimination. Buzzfeed News, 4 April 2019. https://www.buzzfeednews.com/article/tasneemnashrulla/middle-school-teacher-fired-topless-selfie-lawsuit.
5. Ibid.
6. Ibid.
7. VICE News, 2019.
8. Buzzfeed, 2019.
9. VICE News, 2019.
10. Samantha Cole. We Are Truly Fucked: Everyone is Making AI-Generated Fake Porn Now. Vice.com, 24 January 2018. https://www.vice.com/en/article/bjye8a/reddit-fake-porn-app-daisy-ridley
11. John Berger, *Ways of Seeing* (Penguin, 1972).
12. Michel Foucault, 'Panopticism', *Discipline and Punish: The Birth of the Prison* (Penguin, 1991), pp. 195–256.
13. Jeremy Bentham, *The Collected Works of Jeremy Bentham* (William Tait, 1843), p. 37.
14. Foucault, 1991.
15. Alice Marwick. 'The Public Domain: Surveillance in Everyday Life', *Cyber-Surveillance in Everyday Life*, vol. 9, no. 4, 2012.
16. Foucault, 1991.
17. Marwick, 2012.
18. Sophie Davies. Revenge Porn Soars in Europe's Coronavirus Lockdown as Student Fights Back. Reuters.com, 5 May 2020.

https://in.reuters.com/article/us-health-coronavirus-europe-porn-trfn/revenge-porn-soars-in-europes-coronavirus-lockdown-as-student-fights-back-idUSKBN22H2I6.

19. Maeve Duggan. Online Harassment 2017. Pew Research Centre: Internet and Technology, 11 July 2017. https://www.pewresearch.org/internet/2017/07/11/online-harassment-2017.
20. 'Toxic Twitter – a Toxic Place for Women'. Amnesty International, March 2018. https://www.amnesty.org/en/latest/research/2018/03/online-violence-against-women-chapter-1.
21. Sheila Hanlon. 'Lady Cyclist Effigy at the Cambridge University Protest, 1897'. 16 April 2011. https://www.sheilahanlon.com/?p=292.
22. Ibid.
23. Kat Jungnickel. 'Letter from Kitty J. Buckman to Uriah, 23 August 1897', *Bikes and Bloomers: Victorian Women Inventors and their Extraordinary Cycle Wear* (Goldsmiths Press, 2018), p. 11.
24. J. Bailey, V. Steeves, J. Burkell, P. Regan. 'Negotiating with Gender Stereotypes on Social Networking Sites: From "Bicycle Face" to Facebook', *Journal of Communication Inquiry*, 20(10), 2013, 91–112.
25. https://en.wikipedia.org/wiki/Resting_bitch_face.
26. Do YOU have tech face? The weird ways your mobile phone is rapidly ageing your skin (and the clever ways to fix it). Mail Online, 2 August 2016. https://www.dailymail.co.uk/femail/article-3719505/Do-tech-face-weird-ways-mobile-phone-rapidly-ageing-face-clever-ways-fix-it.html.
27. Miss Richardson's Statement, *The Times*, 11 March 1914.
28. Bailey et al., 2013.
29. Adapted from a section in Mary McGill, How the Light Gets In: Notes on the Female Gaze and Selfie Culture. *MAI : Feminism & Visual Culture*, 1 May 2018. https://maifeminism.com/how-the-light-gets-in-notes-on-the-female-gaze-and-selfie-culture.

30. Ibid.
31. Gaye Tuchman. 'Introduction: The Symbolic Annihilation of Women by the Mass Media' in G. Tuchman, A.D. Kaplan, J.B. Walker (eds), *Hearth and Home: Images of Women in the Mass Media* (Oxford University Press, 1978), pp. 3–38.
32. Jessica Carpani, Jack Hardy. L'Oréal boss says Instagram is good for business as young women need to buy make-up to look like filtered selfies. *The Daily Telegraph,* 16 February 2019. https://www.telegraph.co.uk/news/2019/09/16/loreal-boss-says-instagram-good-business-young-women-need-buy.
33. Hanna Kozlowska. Buying Instagram is probably the smartest thing Facebook has ever done. Quartz.com, 25 June 2018. https://qz.com/1314089/instagrams-worth-is-now-estimated-to-be-100-billion.
34. Katharine A. Kaplan. Facemash Creator Survives Ad Board, *The Harvard Crimson*, 19 November 2003. https://www.thecrimson.com/article/2003/11/19/facemash-creator-survives-ad-board-the.
35. Madison Feller. Here's Mark Zuckerberg Testifying Before Congress That Yes, He Really Did Create A Website To Rank Women. *Elle*, 11 April 2018. https://www.elle.com/culture/celebrities/a19746346/mark-zuckerberg-testifying-congress-facesmash-facebook.
36. The Gallery of Beauties, https://en.wikipedia.org/wiki/Gallery_of_Beauties.
37. Berger, 1972.
38. Ibid.
39. Ibid.
40. Patricia Hill Collins. 'Mammies, Matriarchs and Other Controlling Images', *Black Feminist Thought* (Routledge, 2000).
41. Yvonne Kelly, A. Zilanawala, C. Booker, A. Sacker. Social Media Use and Adolescent Mental Health: Findings from the UK Millennium Cohort Study. EClinical Medicine 6 (2018), 59–68.
42. https://www.yourfatfriend.com.

43. Jamie Fullerton and Helen Davidson. You saved Rahaf's life: online outcry kept 'terrified' Saudi woman safe, says friend. *The Guardian*, 8 January 2019. https://www.theguardian.com/world/2019/jan/08/rahaf-al-qunun-saudi-woman-under-un-protection-as-australia-urges-asylum-claim.
44. Heather Chen and Mayuri Mei Lin. Rahar al-Qunun: Unpicking the tweets that may have saved her life. BBC News, 10 January 2019. https://www.bbc.com/news/world-asia-46819199.
45. Lisa Nakamura. 'Afterword: Blaming, Shaming, and the Femininization of Social Media' in Rachel E. Dubrofsky and Shoshana Magnet (eds), *Feminist Surveillance Studies* (Duke University Press, 2015), 221–8.
46. Ben Hubbard. Apple and Google Urged to Dump Saudi App That Lets Men Track Women. *The New York Times*, 13 February 2019. https://www.nytimes.com/2019/02/13/world/middleeast/saudi-arabia-app-women.html.
47. Cohen, 2018.
48. Sir Tim Berners-Lee. Why the web needs to work for girls and women. World Wide Web Foundation, 12 March 2020. https://webfoundation.org/2020/03/web-birthday-31.
49. Ibid.
50. Donna Haraway. 'A Cyborg Manifesto: Science, Technology, and Socialist Feminism in the Late Twentieth Century', *Simians, Cyborgs and Women: The Reinvention of Nature* (Routledge, 1991).

Two: Self/ie

1. Essena O'Neill. 'Why I Really Am Quitting Social Media'. YouTube, 6 November 2015. https://www.youtube.com/watch?v=gmAbwTQvWX8.
2. 'Nosedive'. *Black Mirror*. Episode 1, Series 3. Netflix.
3. Australia Instagram star Essena O'Neill quits 'unhealthy' social media. BBC News, 3 November 2015. https://www.bbc.com/news/world-australia-34707116?piano-modal.

4. Elizabeth Losh. 'Feminism Reads Big Data: "Social Physics," Atomism, and *Selfiecity*', *International Journal of Communication,* USC Annenberg, vol. 9 (2015), 1647–59.
5. Frances Borzello, *Seeing Ourselves: Women's Self-Portraits* (Thames & Hudson, 1998).
6. Ibid.
7. Joan Riviere, 'Womanliness as a masquerade', *The International Journal of Psychoanalysis 10* (1929), 303–13.
8. Simone de Beauvoir, *The Second Sex* (Vintage, 2010).
9. Ibid.
10. Ibid.
11. Jean M. Twenge and W. Keith Campbell, *The Narcissism Epidemic: Living in the Age of Entitlement* (Atria Books, 2010).
12. Christopher Lasch, *The Culture of Narcissism: American Life in an Age of Diminishing Expectations* (W.W. Norton & Co., 1979).
13. Mary McGill. We're all celebrities now, *RTÉ Brainstorm*, 7 December 2018. https://www.rte.ie/brainstorm/2018/1206/1015607-were-all-celebrities-now.
14. Alice E. Marwick, *Status Update: Celebrity, Publicity, and Branding in the Social Media Age* (Yale University Press, 2013).
15. Daniel Halpern, S. Valenzuela, J.E. Katz. '"Selfie-ists" or "Narci-selfiers"? A Cross-Lagged Panel of Selfie-Taking and Narcissism', *Personality and Individual Differences*, vol. 97 (2016), 98–101.
16. Phil Reed, N.I. Bircek, L.A. Osborne, C. Vigano, R. Truzoli. 'Visual Social Media Moderates the Relationship between Initial Problematic Internet Use and Later Narcissism', *The Open Psychology Journal*, 2018, 163–170.
17. E.A. Koterba, F. Ponti, K. Ligman. '"Get out of my selfie!" Narcissism, gender, and motives for self-photography among emerging adults', *Psychology of Popular Media*, 2021 10 (1), 98–104.
18. Piotr Sorokowski, A. Sorokowska, A. Oleszkiewicz, T. Frackowiak, A. Huk, K. Pisanski. 'Selfie posting behaviors are associated with

narcissism among men', *Personality and Individual Differences*, vol. 85 (2015), 123–7.

19. Anne Burns. 'Self(ie)-Discipline: Social Regulation as Enacted Through the Discussion of Photographic Practice', *International Journal of Communication*, USC Annenberg, vol. 9 (2015), 1716–33.
20. M.N. West, '"Proudly Displayed by Wearers of Chic Ensembles": Vanity Cameras, Kodak Girls, and the Culture of Female Fashion', *Kodak and the Lens of Nostalgia* (University of Virginia Press, 2000), pp. 109–35.
21. Lance Ulanoff. Does Instagram Owe Kodak a Billion Dollar Thanks? MashableUK, 10 April 2012. https://mashable.com/2012/04/10/what-does-instagram-owe-kodak/?europe=true.
22. Syreeta McFadden. Selfies allow black women to say we are here, and we are beautiful. *The Guardian*, 24 February 2015. https://www.theguardian.com/commentisfree/2015/feb/24/selfies-black-women-we-are-here-we-are-beautiful.
23. Mehita Iqani, 'Celebrity Skin: Race, Gender and the Politics of Feminine Beauty in Celebrity Selfies', *Consumption, Media and the Global South* (Palgrave Macmillan, 2016), pp.160–95.
24. Annabel Rackham. Disability blogger: 'Trolls said I was too ugly for selfies so I hit back'. BBC News, 11 September 2019. https://www.bbc.com/news/newsbeat-49662140.
25. #BBCTrending: The women having a laugh in Turkey. BBC News, 29 July 2014. https://www.bbc.com/news/blogs-trending-28548179.
26. Claire Lampen. What Is 'Challenge Accepted', Exactly? *The Cut*, 29 July 2020. https://www.thecut.com/2020/07/what-is-womensupportingwomen-challengeaccepted.html.
27. Matt Southern. Gains From Recent Social Media Spikes. Seachenginejournal.com, 27 April 2020. https://www.searchenginejournal.com/instagram-growth-in-2020/364490/#close.

28. Naomi Wolf, *The Beauty Myth* (Vintage, 1991).
29. Ibid.
30. Sandra Lee Bartky, *Femininity and Domination: Studies in the Phenomenology of Oppression* (Routledge, 1990).
31. Laura Mulvey. 'Visual Pleasure and Narrative Cinema', *Screen*, vol. 16, issue 3 (1975), 6–18.
32. Jill Walker Rettberg, *Seeing Ourselves Through Technology: How We Use Selfies, Blogs and Wearable Devices to See and Shape Ourselves* (Palgrave Macmillan, 2014).
33. Marcia Belsky. The Headless Women of Hollywood. http://www.marciabelsky.com/the-headless-women-of-hollywood.
34. Jean Kilbourne, *Can't Buy ME Love: How Advertising Changes the Way We Think and Feel* (Prentice Hall & IBD, 2000).
35. Tavi Gevinson. Who Would I Be Without Instagram? An investigation. *The Cut*, 16 September 2019. https://www.thecut.com/2019/09/who-would-tavi-gevinson-be-without-instagram.html.
36. Jennifer S. Mills, S. Musto, L. Williams, M. Tiggemann. '"Selfie" harm: Effects on mood and body image in young women', *Body Image*, vol. 28 (2018), 86–92.
37. Ibid.
38. Marika Tiggemann, Isabella Anderberg, Zoe Brown. 'Uploading your best self: Selfie editing and body dissatisfaction', *Body Image*, vol. 33 (2020), 175–82.
39. Rachel Cohen, T. Newton-John, A. Slater. "Selfie"-objectification: The role of selfies in self-objectification and disordered eating in young women', *Computers in Human Behavior*, vol. 79 (2018), 68–94.
40. Amelia C. Couture Bue. 'The looking glass selfie: Instagram use frequency predicts visual attention to high-anxiety body regions in young women', *Computers in Human Behavior*, vol. 108 (2020).
41. Ibid.

42. Sophia J. Lamp, A. Cugle, A.L. Silverman, M. Thomas, M. Liss, M.J. Erchull. 'Picture Perfect: The Relationship Between Selfie Behaviors, Self-Objectification, and Depressive Symptoms', *Sex Roles*, vol. 81 (2019), 704–12.
43. Jasmine Fardouly and Ronald M. Rapee. 'The impact of no-makeup selfies on young women's body image', *Body Image*, vol. 28 (2019), 128–34.
44. Marika Tiggemann and Mia Zaccardo. '"Exercise to be fit, not skinny": The effect of fitspiration imagery on women's body image', *Body Image*, vol. 15 (2015), 61–7.
45. Celeste Barber, Instagram, 2020. Instagram.com/CelesteBarber.
46. Instagram Reality Baybeh! Reddit, 2020. https://www.reddit.com/r/Instagramreality.
47. Marika Tiggemann and Isabella Anderberg. 'Social media is not real: The effect of "Instagram vs reality" on women's social comparison and body image', *New Media & Society*, 2019. https://doi.org/10.1177/1461444819888720.
48. Rankin, Selfie Harm (2019). https://www.instagram.com/rankinarchive.
49. Ibid.
50. I Got Surgery to Look Like my Snapchat and Facetune Selfie. VICE Asia, 2019. https://www.youtube.com/watch?v=f5fCt1twyKo.
51. McFadden, 2015.
52. Tiffany Ferguson. The Return of Essena O'Neill – interview with Instagram model who quit social media (2019). https://www.youtube.com/watch?v=Ce5kkO_urHE.
53. Essena O'Neill, Authority Within (2020). https://www.authoritywithin.com.
54. Essena O'Neill, Instagram (2020). https://www.instagram.com/essenaoneill.

Three: Bodies

1. Petra Collins. Why Instagram Censored My Body, *Huffington Post*, 6 December 2013. https://www.huffpost.com/entry/why-instagram-censored-my-body_b_4118416.
2. Ibid.
3. Ibid.
4. Ibid.
5. Ibid.
6. https://about.instagram.com.
7. Hannah Seligson. Why Are More Women Than Men on Instagram? *The Atlantic*, 7 June 2016. https://www.theatlantic.com/technology/archive/2016/06/why-are-more-women-than-men-on-instagram/485993/.
8. Who Runs The World? Female Instagram users get five times more likes on average than men. HopperHQ.com, 14 March 2017. https://www.hopperhq.com/blog/runs-world-female-instagram-users-get-five-times-likes-average-men.
9. Ibid.
10. Jenna Drenten, Lauren Gurrieri, Meagan Tyler. How highly sexualised imagery is shaping 'influence' on Instagram – and harassment is rife, *The Conversation*, 7 May 2019. https://theconversation.com/how-highly-sexualised-imagery-is-shaping-influence-on-instagram-and-harassment-is-rife-113030.
11. Laura Mulvey. 'Visual Pleasure and Narrative Cinema', *Screen*, vol.16, issue 3, 1975, 6–18.
12. Susan Bordo, *Twilight Zones: The Hidden Life of Cultural Images from Plato to O.J.* (University of California Press, 1999), p. 114.
13. Nosheen Iqbal. Instagram 'censorship' of black model's photo reignites claims of race bias. *The Observer*, 9 August 2020. https://www.theguardian.com/technology/2020/aug/09/instagrams-censorship-of-black-models-photo-shoot-reignites-claims-of-race-bias-nyome-nicholas-williams.

14. Ibid.
15. Ibid.
16. Ibid.
17. Adam Mosseri, Twitter.com, 15 June 2020. https://twitter.com/mosseri/status/1272592293111848962?lang=en.
18. bell hooks, 'Selling Hot Pussy: Representations of Black Female Sexuality in the Cultural Marketplace', *Black Looks: Race and Representation* (South End Press, 1992), pp. 61–78.
19. Sameer Suri. Kylie Jenner goes TOPLESS in hat and veil for smouldering new shoot … after celebrating 23rd birthday. 11 August 2020. https://www.dailymail.co.uk/tvshowbiz/article-8617023/Kylie-Jenner-goes-TOPLESS-hat-veil-smoldering-new-shoot-celebrating-23rd-birthday.html.
20. A. Sastre. 'Hottentot in the age of reality TV: sexuality, race, and Kim Kardashian's visible body', *Celebrity Studies*, 5 (1–2) (2014), 123–37.
21. Amanda Fortini. Break the Internet: Kim Kardashian. *Paper*, 12 November 2014. https://www.papermag.com/break-the-internet-kim-kardashian-cover-1427450475.html.
22. Suyin Haynes. What Links Kim Kardashian to the Victorians? *LSE Undergraduate Political Review*, 26 October 2016. https://blogs.lse.ac.uk/lseupr/2016/10/26/what-links-kim-kardashian-to-the-victorians.
23. Proceedings of the Academy of Sciences of the Royal Institute of France. *The Journal of Science and the Arts* (1818, III (V)) 154.
24. Sadiah Qureshi. 'Displaying Sara Baartman, the "Hottentot Venus"', *History of Science* 42.2 (2004), 233–57.
25. Bernhard Debatin, J.P. Lovejoy, A-K. Horn, B.N. Hughes. 'Facebook and online privacy: attitudes, behaviors, and unintended consequences', *Journal of Computer-Mediated Communication*, 15(1) (2009), 83–108.
26. Safiya Umoja Noble, *Algorithms of Oppression: How Search Engines Reinforce Racism* (New York University Press, 2018)

27. Cathy O'Neil, *Weapons of Math Destruction* (Penguin, 2016).
28. Sara Wachter-Boettcher, *Technically Wrong: Sexist Apps, Biased Algorithms, and Other Threats of Toxic Tech* (W.W. Norton & Co., 2017).
29. Noble, 2018, p. 6, p. 71.
30. Tama Leaver, Tim Highfield, Crystal Abidin, *Instagram: Visual Social Media Cultures* (Polity, 2020).
31. Casey Newton. Facebook will pay $52 million in settlement with moderators who developed PTSD on the job, *The Verge*, 12 May 2020. https://www.theverge.com/2020/5/12/21255870/facebook-content-moderator-settlement-scola-ptsd-mental-health.
32. Leaver et al., 2020.
33. Ibid.
34. Jennifer Savin. How Instagram is going to stop censoring plus size Black women, Cosmopolitan.com, 24 August 2020. https://www.cosmopolitan.com/uk/body/health/a33747909/instagram-censoring-plus-size-black-women.
35. Josh Constine. Instagram now demotes vaguely 'inappropriate' content. *Techcrunch*, 10 April 2020. https://techcrunch.com/2019/04/10/instagram-borderline.
36. Ibid.
37. Instagram, please stop censoring pole dance. Change.org.
38. Carolina Are. Instagram Apologises to Pole Dancers About the Shadowban. 31 July 2019. https://bloggeronpole.com/2019/07/instagram-apologises-to-pole-dancers-about-the-shadowban.
39. https://everybodyvisible.com/about-us/.
40. Adam Mosseri, Twitter, 22 February 2020. https://twitter.com/jackierauts/status/1231122961379340289.
41. Radhika Sanghani. 'Get 'em up there girls!' – all hail the new taboo-busting Tampax advert, *The Telegraph*, 15 April 2020. https://www.telegraph.co.uk/women/life/get-em-girls-hail-new-taboo-busting-tampax-advert.

42. Ibid.
43. Laura Lynott. 'Offensive, crude and over-descriptive' Tampax ad banned after 84 complaints, *Independent.ie*, 29 July 2020. https://www.independent.ie/irish-news/offensive-crude-and-over-descriptive-tampax-ad-banned-after-84-complaints-39408354.html.
44. RTÉ.ie. Complaints over tampon ad upheld by Advertising Standards Authenticity, 29 July 2020. https://www.rte.ie/news/2020/0729/1156264-tampon-advertising-complaint, accessed 4 September 2020.
45. 'State of the Period – The widespread impact of period poverty on US students', white paper. https://cdn.shopify.com/s/files/1/0795/1599/files/State-of-the-Period-white-paper_Thinx_PERIOD.pdf?455788.
46. Ibid.
47. Rupi Kaur, Instagram.com. https://www.instagram.com/p/0ovWwJHA6f/?utm_source=ig_embed.
48. Zing Tsjeng. Why Instagram censored this image of an artist on her period. dazeddigital.com, 27 March 2015. https://www.dazeddigital.com/artsandculture/article/24258/1/why-instagram-censored-this-image-of-an-artist-on-her-period.
49. Ibid.
50. Ibid.
51. Ibid.
52. Judy Chicago, *Womanhouse, Menstruation Bathroom* (site installation, 1972). http://dome.mit.edu/handle/1721.3/2403.
53. Ibid.
54. Joan Smith, *Misogynies* (The Westbourne Press, 2013).
55. Julia Kristeva, *Powers of Horror: An Essay on Abjection* (Columbia University Press, 1982).
56. Amy Slater, Natasha Cole, Jasmine Fardouly. 'The effect of exposure to parodies of thin-ideal images on young women's body image and mood', *Body Image*, vol. 29 (2019), 82–9.

57. Lacey-Jade Christie. Instagram censored one of these images but not the other. We must ask why. *The Guardian*, 19 October 2020. https://www.theguardian.com/technology/2020/oct/20/instagram-censored-one-of-these-photos-but-not-the-other-we-must-ask-why.
58. Ibid.
59. Ibid.
60. Essena O'Neill. 'Why I Really Am Quitting Social Media'. YouTube, 6 November 2015. https://www.youtube.com/watch?v=gmAbwTQvWX8.
61. Nicola Döring, Anne Reif, Sandra Poeschl. 'How gender-typical are selfies? A content analysis and comparison with magazine adverts', *Computers in Human Behavior* (2015, 55 (2016)), 955–62.
62. Jasmine Fardouly, Brydie K. Willburger, Lenny R. Vartanian. 'Instagram use and young women's body image concerns and self-objectification: Testing mediational pathways', *New Media & Society* (2017 20(4)), 1380–95.
63. Kayla Logan. Don't Delete My Body, kaylalogan.com, 1 October 2020. https://kaylalogan.com/dont-delete-my-body.
64. Nosheen Iqbal. Instagram row over plus-size model forces change to nudity policy. *The Guardian*, 25 October 2020. https://www.theguardian.com/technology/2020/oct/25/instagram-row-over-plus-size-model-forces-change-to-nudity-policy.
65. Monica Heisey. Meet the Woman Running an Instagram Devoted to Menstrual Blood. Vice.com, 21 September 2015. https://www.vice.com/en_us/article/a3ww5z/meet-the-woman-running-an-instagram-devoted-to-menstrual-blood.
66. Ibid.
67. Corporate Human Rights Policy. Facebook.com. March 2021.https://about.fb.com/wp-content/uploads/2021/03/Facebooks-Corporate-Human-Rights-Policy.pdf

68. Adam Mosseri. An Update on Our Equity Work. Instagram.com. September 2020. https://about.instagram.com/blog/announcements/updates-on-our-equity-work
69. Ibid.
70. https://help.instagram.com/313829416281232
71. Mosseri, 2020.
72. Instagram.com https://about.instagram.com.

Four: Influence

1. N. Robehmed. At 21, Kylie Jenner Becomes the Youngest Self-Made Billionaire Ever, forbes.com. https://www.forbes.com/sites/natalierobehmed/2019/03/05/at-21-kylie-jenner-becomes-the-youngest-self-made-billionaire-ever/#337790bb2794.
2. Roxane Gay. Quoted in Alex Abad-Santos, The Controversy Over 'Kylie Jenner, Self-Made Billionaire,' Explained. vox.com. https://www.vox.com/2018/7/13/17568328/kylie-jenner-billionaire-forbes-backlash.
3. 'Kylie Jenner: From Lip Kits To A $900 Million Fortune In Just 3 Years', forbes.com, 2018. https://www.youtube.com/watch?v=pCv7jY-5STE.
4. Chapter opening adapted from Mary McGill. 'Selfie-Surveillance: Exploring Postfeminist-Neoliberal Visibility in Young Women's Selfie-Practices.' Unpublished PhD thesis, National University of Ireland, Galway, April 2020.
5. Elaine Lipworth. Khloé Kardashian: Our denim's all about empowerment, making women feel great. *Belfast Telegraph*, 2017. https://www.belfasttelegraph.co.uk/life/weekend/khloe-kardashian-our-denims-all-about-empowerment-making-the-women-feel-great-35636005.html
6. Influencer Marketing: Social Media Influencer Market Stats and Research for 2021. Businessinsider.com, 2021. https://www.businessinsider.com/influencer-marketing-report.

7. Amelia Tait. 'Influencers are being taken advantage of': the social media stars turning to unions. *The Guardian*, 10 October 2020. https://www.theguardian.com/media/2020/oct/10/influencers-are-being-taken-advantage-of-the-stars-turning-to-unions.
8. Vuelio, UK Bloggers Survey 2019. https://www.vuelio.com/uk/wp-content/uploads/2019/03/UK-Bloggers-Survey-2019.pdf.
9. Inzpire.me. #WhitePaper: Peeking behind the influencer curtain to mark the 10th anniversary of Instagram in 2020. https://blog.inzpire.me/wp-content/uploads/2019/12/inzpireme-Whitepaper.pdf.
10. Lauren Berlant, *Cruel Optimism* (Duke University Press, 2011).
11. *Everything Is Copy – Nora Ephron: Scripted & Unscripted* (movie), Loveless, 2016.
12. Jia Tolentino. The Age of Instagram Face, *The New Yorker*, 12 December 2019. https://www.newyorker.com/culture/decade-in-review/the-age-of-instagram-face.
13. Ibid.
14. Ibid.
15. Simone de Beauvoir, *The Second Sex* (Vintage, 2010).
16. Alice Leppert. 'Keeping Up with the Kardashians: Fame-Work and the Production of Entrepreneurial Sisterhood' in E. Levine (ed.), *Cupcakes, Pinterest, and Ladyporn: Feminized Popular Culture in the Early Twenty-First Century* (University of Illinois Press, 2015), pp. 215–31.
17. Alison Harvey. 'The Fame Game: Working Your Way Up the Celebrity Ladder in *Kim Kardashian: Hollywood*', *Games and Culture*, 21 February 2018, 1–19.
18. Sheryl Sandberg, *Lean In: Women, Work, and the Will to Lead* (W.H. Allen, 2015).
19. Sophia Amoruso, *#GirlBoss* (Penguin, 2015).

20. Sam Biddle, Paulo Victor Ribeiro, Tatiana Dias. Invisible Censorship: TikTok Moderators to Suppress Posts By 'Ugly' People and the Poor to Attract New Users, *The Intercept*, 16 March 2020. https://theintercept.com/2020/03/16/tiktok-app-moderators-users-discrimination.
21. Alison Winch, *Girlfriends and Postfeminist Sisterhood* (Palgrave Macmillan, 2013).
22. Ibid.
23. Jia Tolentino, *Trick Mirror: Reflections On Self-Delusion* (4th Estate, 2019).
24. Ibid.
25. Verity Johnson. The empty world of the influencer. Stuff.co.nz, 23 May 2020. https://www.stuff.co.nz/life-style/300011835/the-empty-world-of-the-influencer.
26. Brooke Erin Duffy, *(Not) Getting Paid to Do What You Love: Gender, Social Media and Aspirational Work* (Yale University Press, 2017).
27. Ibid.
28. Tolentino, 2019.
29. Global Wellness Economy Monitor. GlobalWellnessInstitute.com. 2018. https://globalwellnessinstitute.org/industry-research/2018-global-wellness-economy-monitor/
30. Susie Orbach, *Bodies* (Profile Books, 2019).
31. Ibid.
32. Audre Lorde, *A Burst of Light and Other Essays* (Firebrand Books, 1988), pp. 49–134.
33. Helen Fielding, *Bridget Jones's Diary* (Picador, 1996).
34. Chase Peterson-Withorn, Madeline Berg. Inside Kylie Jenner's Web of Lies – And Why She is No Longer a Billionaire. *Forbes*, June 2020. https://www.forbes.com/sites/chasewithorn/2020/05/29/inside-kylie-jennerss-web-of-lies-and-why-shes-no-longer-a-billionaire/?sh=6cfbd125f7b8.
35. Ibid.
36. Sam Blum. The fatigue hitting influencers as Instagram evolves, BBC News, 21 October 2019. https://www.bbc.com/worklife/

article/20191022-the-fatigue-hitting-influencers-as-instagram-evolves.

37. Adele Walton. I thought I had a healthy approach to influencing – then The Social Dilemma gave me the reality check I needed. Independent.co.uk, 21 September 2020. https://www.independent.co.uk/voices/digital-burnout-social media-dilemma-netflix-influencing-instagram-b511663.html.
38. Kimberly Truong. Kim Kardashian Reportedly 'Doesn't Care' That You Were Mad About Her Birthday Party. *InStyle*, 30 October 2020. https://www.instyle.com/celebrity/kim-kardashian-west/kim-kardashian-birthday-backlash-response.
39. Lauren Cochrane. Perfect storm: have the influencers selling a dream lost their allure? *The Observer*, 6 February 2021. https://www.theguardian.com/media/2021/feb/06/perfect-storm-have-the-influencers-selling-a-dream-lost-their-allure.
40. Ibid.
41. Deepa Mahajan, Olivia White, Anu Magdavkar, Mekala Kirshnan. Don't Let the Pandemic Set Back Gender Equality. *Harvard Business Review*, 16 September 2020. https://hbr.org/2020/09/dont-let-the-pandemic-set-back-gender-equality.
42. Jennifer O'Connell. Kim Kardashian West didn't invent body shaming, but she is building an empire out of it. *The Irish Times*, 14 September 2020. https://www.irishtimes.com/life-and-style/fashion/kim-kardashian-west-didn-t-invent-body-shaming-but-she-is-building-an-empire-out-of-it-1.4354453.

Five: Misogyny 2.0

1. Rory Carroll. Reddit bans groups behind sharing of leaked celebrity photos. *The Guardian*, 7 September 2014. https://www.theguardian.com/technology/2014/sep/07/reddit-bans-groups-behind-sharing-of-leaked-celebrity-photos.
2. Ibid.
3. Lena Dunham, Twitter.com, 2014. https://twitter.com/lenadunham/status/506399334146256896?lang=en.

4. Cover Exclusive: Jennifer Lawrence Calls Photo Hacking a 'Sex Crime'. *Vanity Fair*, 7 October 2014. https://www.vanityfair.com/hollywood/2014/10/jennifer-lawrence-cover.
5. Amanda Hess. Inside AnonIB, Where Hacking Is a Sport and Women's Bodies Are the Prize. Slate.com, 3 September 2014. https://slate.com/human-interest/2014/09/anonib-nude-photo-site-where-hackers-and-users-treat-women-as-property.html.
6. Ibid.
7. Ibid.
8. Kate Manne, *Down Girl: The Logic of Misogyny* (Penguin, 2018).
9. Michael Salter. Privates in the online public: Sex(ting) and reputation on social media. 2015, New Media & Society. https://doi.org/10.1177/1461444815604133.
10. Laura Mulvey. 'Visual Pleasure and Narrative Cinema', *Screen*, vol. 16, issue 3, 1975, 6–18.
11. Emma A. Jane. 'Gendered cyberhate as workplace harassment and economic vandalism', *Feminist Media Studies*, 2018.
12. Azmina Dhrodia. Unsocial Media: Tracking Twitter Abuse Against Women MPs. *Amnesty Global Insights*, Medium.com, 4 September 2017. https://medium.com/@AmnestyInsights/unsocial media-tracking-twitter-abuse-against-women-mps-fc28aeca498a.
13. Ibid.
14. https://fixtheglitch.org.
15. Amnesty International. Women abused on Twitter every 30 seconds – new study. Press release, 18 December 2018. https://www.amnesty.org.uk/press-releases/women-abused-twitter-every-30-seconds-new-study.
16. Jessica Megarry. Under the watchful eyes of men: theorising the implications of male surveillance practices for feminist activism on social media, *Feminist Media Studies*, 2017.
17. Angela Nagle, *Kill All Normies: Online Culture Wars from 4chan and Tumblr to Trump and the Alt-Right* (Zero Books, 2017).

18. Emma A. Jane. Online Abuse and Harassment, *The International Encyclopaedia of Gender, Media, and Communication*, March 2020.
19. Becky Gardiner. 'It's a terrible way to go to work:' what 70 million readers' comments on *The Guardian* revealed about hostility to women and minorities online, *Feminist Media Studies*, vol. 18, 22 March 2018, 592–608.
20. Clare McGlynn and Erika Rackley. 'Image-Based Sexual Abuse', *Oxford Journal of Legal Studies*, 37(3), 31 January 2017, 534–61.
21. Liz Kelly. The Continuum of Sexual Violence in Hanmer J., Maynard M. (eds), *Women, Violence and Social Control. Explorations in Sociology* (British Sociological Association Conference volume series, 1987). Palgrave Macmillan, London.
22. Anastasia Powell, Asher Flynn. Report of 'revenge porn' skyrocketed during lockdown, we must stop blaming victims for it. RMIT Australia, 3 June 2020. https://www.rmit.edu.au/news/all-news/2020/jun/revenge-porn-during-covid.
23. https://notyourporn.com.
24. The 2019 Year in Review. 11 December 2019. Pornhub.com/Insights. https://www.pornhub.com/insights/2019-year-in-review.
25. The Tech Companies That Have Had the Biggest Impact on Society in the 21st Century. Diggitymarketing.com,. https://diggitymarketing.com/most-influential-tech-companies-2020.
26. Pornhub, 2019.
27. Nicholas Kristof. The Children of Pornhub, *The New York Times*, 4 December 2020. https://www.nytimes.com/2020/12/04/opinion/sunday/pornhub-rape-trafficking.html.
28. Russell Brandon. Pornhub limits uploads and disables downloads after New York Times exposé. TheVerge.com, 8 December 2020. https://www.theverge.com/2020/12/8/22164031/pornhub-upload-limit-blocked-download-nyt-kristof-child-abuse.
29. Siladitya Ray. Pornhub Takes Down All Content Uploaded By Unverified Users. Forbes.com, 14 December 2020.

https://www.forbes.com/sites/siladityaray/2020/12/14/pornhub-takes-down-all-content-uploaded-by-unverified-uploaders/?sh=2190221065ed.

30. Ellen Fitzpatrick. Woman goes viral with fake app for reporting unsolicited dick pics to police. Evoke.ie, 5 February 2020. https://evoke.ie/2020/02/05/extra/woman-fake-app-dick-pics-police.
31. https://www.instagram.com/byefelipe.
32. Erin Lindsay. New survey finds 88% of women have been harassed while using dating apps. Image.ie., 5 March 2020. https://www.image.ie/uncategorized/new-survey-finds-88-women-harassed-using-dating-apps-182874.
33. Mansoor Iqbal. Tinder Revenue and Usage Statistics (2020), Business of Apps, 30 October 2020. https://www.businessofapps.com/data/tinder-statistics.
34. *Swiped: Hooking-Up in the Digital Age*, HBO, 2018. https://www.hbo.com/documentaries/swiped-hooking-up-in-the-digital-age.
35. Jessica Strubel, Trent A. Petrie. 'Love Me Tinder: Body image and psychosocial functioning among men and women', *Body Image*, vol. 21, 2017, 34–8.
36. Monica Anderson, Emily A. Vogels, Erica Turner. The Virtues and Downsides of Online Dating. Pew Research Centre, 6 February 2020: https://www.pewresearch.org/internet/2020/02/06/the-virtues-and-downsides-of-online-dating.
37. Ibid.
38. Iqbal, 2020.
39. Karen McVeigh. Cyberstalking 'now more common' than face-to-face' stalking. *The Guardian*, 1 April 2011. https://www.theguardian.com/uk/2011/apr/08/cyberstalking-study-victims-men.
40. Jamie Grierson. Surge in stalking victims seeking help during UK lockdown. *The Guardian*, 8 May 2020. https://www.

theguardian.com/uk-news/2020/may/08/coronavirus-surge-stalking-victims-seeking-help-during-uk-lockdown.
41. Ibid.
42. Cherry Wilson. Stalking: My ex-partner sent me 4,000 emails. BBC News, 19 May 2020. https://www.bbc.com/news/uk-52730367.
43. Ibid.
44. https://www.womensaid.ie/help/coercive-control.html.
45. Rosanna Bellini, Emily Tseng, Nora McDonald, Rachel Greenstadt, Damon McCoy, Thomas Ristenpart, Nicola Dell. 'So-called privacy breeds evil': Narrative Justifications for Intimate Partner Surveillance in Online Forums. Proceedings of the ACM on Human-Computer Interactions, January 2021. https://dl.acm.org/doi/abs/10.1145/3432909.
46. Nana Baah. After My Ex Stalked Me Online, I Saw The Dark Side Of Romantic Obsession. Vice.com, 24 July 2018. https://www.vice.com/en/article/8xbgg4/ex-boyfriend-cyberstalking-victim-essay.
47. Ibid.
48. https://www.instagram.com/instagranniepants/?hl=en.
49. Margaret Atwood, *Second Words: Selected Critical Prose 1962–1980* (Anansi Press, 2018), p. 413.
50. Angela Nagle. The New Man of 4chan. *The Baffler*, March 2016, no. 30. https://thebaffler.com/salvos/new-man-4chan-nagle.

Six: Change

1. Benjamin Haas. 'Escape the Corset': South Korean women rebel against strict beauty standards. *The Guardian*, 26 October 2018. https://www.theguardian.com/world/2018/oct/26/escape-the-corset-south-korean-women-rebel-against-strict-beauty-standards.
2. Escape the Corset: The South Korean Feminist Campaign You Need to Know About. *Verve*, 12 January 2019. https://

medium.com/verve-up/escape-the-corset-the-south-korean-feminist-campaign-you-need-to-know-about-fe024de6d106.

3. Haas, 2018.
4. Rebecca Crosby. 22,000 People Marched in South Korea Over the Weekend for Women's Rights. Studybreaks.com, 12 June 2018. https://studybreaks.com/thoughts/south-korea-women-march-for-justice.
5. Laura Bicker. Why women in South Korea are cutting 'the corset'. BBC News, 10 December 2018. https://www.bbc.com/news/world-asia-46478449.
6. Jaron Lanier, *Ten Arguments for Deleting Your Social Media Accounts Right Now* (The Bodley Head, 2018).
7. Channel 4 News. Jaron Lanier interview on how social media ruins your life, 15 June 2018. https://www.youtube.com/watch?v=kc_Jq42Og7Q.
8. Whitney Philips and Ryan M. Milner, *The Ambivalent Internet: Mischief, Oddity, and Antagonism Online* (Polity Press, 2017).
9. David Shaw. 'Facebook's flawed emotion experiment: Antisocial research on social network users'. *Research Ethics*, vol. 12, issue 1, January 2016, 29–34. https://journals.sagepub.com/doi/epub/10.1177/1747016115579535.
10. Emilio Ferrara, Zeyao Yang. 'Measuring Emotional Contagion in Social Media'. PLOS ONE 10(11), 6 November 2015. https://doi.org/10.1371/journal.pone.0142390.
11. A.K. Przybylski, K. Murayama, C.R. Dehaan, V. Gladwell, 'Motivational, emotional, and behavioral correlates of fear of missing out'. *Computers in Human Behavior*, 29 (4), July 2013, 1841–8.
12. Richard Seymour, *The Twittering Machine* (The Indigo Press, 2019).
13. Ibid.
14. Nathaniel Branden, *The Six Pillars of Self-Esteem* (Bantam, 1994).

15. James Williams. Technology is Driving Us to Distraction. *The Guardian*, 17 May 2018. https://www.theguardian.com/commentisfree/2018/may/27/world-distraction-demands-new-focus.
16. *Ingrid Goes West* (2017). Star Thrower Entertainment, 141 Entertainment, Mighty Engine.
17. Carrie Goldberg, *Nobody's Victim: Fighting Harassment Online & Off* (Virago, 2019).
18. Ibid.
19. Hemant Taneja. The Era of 'Move Fast and Break Things' Is Over. *Harvard Business Review*, 22 January 2019. https://hbr.org/2019/01/the-era-of-move-fast-and-break-things-is-over.
20. Clare McGlynn and Erika Rackley. 'Image-Based Sexual Abuse'. *Oxford Journal of Legal Studies*, 37(3), 31 January 2017, 534–61.
21. Emma A. Jane. *Misogyny Online: A Short (and Brutish) History* (SAGE Swifts, 2016).
22. https://oversightboard.com.
23. Michelle Bachelet. Human rights in the digital age – Can they make a difference? Ohchr.org, 17 December 2019. https://www.ohchr.org/EN/NewsEvents/Pages/DisplayNews.aspx?NewsID=25158&LangID=E.
24. Ibid.
25. UN experts stress links between digital space and human rights at RightsCon, Tunis. Ohchr.org. 13 June 2019. https://www.ohchr.org/EN/NewsEvents/Pages/DisplayNews.aspx?NewsID=24696.
26. Gender Rights Online. Geneva Internet Platform. https://dig.watch/issues/gender-rights-online.
27. Ibid.
28. Nicolas Suzor, Molly Dragiewicz, Bridget Harris, Rosalie Gillett, Jean Burgess, Tess Van Geelen. Human Rights by Design: The Responsibilities of Social Media Platforms to Address

Gender-Based Violence Online. *Policy & Internet*, 2018. https://onlinelibrary.wiley.com/doi/abs/10.1002/poi3.185.
29. Guiding Principles on Business and Human Rights. Ohchr.org. https://www.ohchr.org/documents/publications/guidingprinciplesbusinesshr_en.pdf.
30. Rosalie Gillett and Nicolas Suzor. Tinder fails to protect women from abuse. But when we brush off 'dick pics' as a laugh, so do we. *The Conversation*, 13 October 2020. https://theconversation.com/tinder-fails-to-protect-women-from-abuse-but-when-we-brush-off-dick-pics-as-a-laugh-so-do-we-147909.
31. Ibid.
32. https://www.accessnow.org/facebook-human-rights-policy/
33. Facebook's Corporate Human Rights Policy. March 2021.
34. https://about.fb.com/wp-content/uploads/2021/03/Facebooks-Corporate-Human-Rights-Policy.pdf.
35. Detecting Non-Consensual Intimate Images and Supporting Images. Facebook Newsroom, 15 March 2019.https://about.fb.com/news/2019/03/detecting-non-consensual-intimate-images.
36. Ibid.
37. Making Facebook a Safer, More Welcoming Place for Women. Facebook Newsroom, 29 October 2019. https://about.fb.com/news/2019/10/inside-feed-womens-safety.
38. Rebecca Jennings. Instagram is Broken. It Also Broke Us. Vox.com, 2 December 2019. https://www.vox.com/the-goods/2019/12/2/20983760/instagram-removing-likes-authenticity.
39. Adrienne So. Instagram Will Test Hiding 'Likes' in the US Starting Next Week. Wired.com, 11 August 2019. https://www.wired.com/story/instagram-hiding-likes-adam-mosseri-tracee-ellis-ross-wired25.
40. Instagram tightens rules on diet and cosmetic surgery post. *The Guardian*, 18 September 2019. https://www.theguardian.com/technology/2019/sep/18/instagram-tightens-rules-on-diet-and-cosmetic-surgery-posts.

Afterword

1. Lisa Finn. 'Victory' For Teacher Fired Over Topless Selfie. Patch.com, 26 May 2020. https://patch.com/new-york/shirley-mastic/victory-teacher-who-says-she-was-fired-topless-selfie.
2. Ibid.
3. Orla Dwyer. Garda Commissioner says 10,000 images examined but no formal complains of image-based abuse made. *The Journal*, 25 November 2020. https://www.thejournal.ie/image-based-sexual-abuse-formal-complaints-10000-pictures-5279047-Nov2020.
4. Ibid.
5. Samantha Cole, Emanuel Maiberg, Anna Koslerova. 'Frankenstein's Monster:' Images of Sexual Abuse Are Fueling Algorithmic Porn. Motherboard, Vice.com, 10 November 2020. https://www.vice.com/en/article/akdgnp/sexual-abuse-fueling-ai-porn-deepfake-czech-casting-girls-do-porn.
6. Abuse and Harassment Driving Girls off Facebook, Instagram and Twitter. Plan International, 5 October 2020. https://plan-international.org/news/2020-10-05-abuse-and-harassment-driving-girls-facebook-instagram-and-twitter.
7. UN Committee Calls for Crackdown on Trafficking of Women and Girls in Digital Age. Committee on the Elimination of Discrimination Against Women and Girls (CEDAW), United Nations, 11 November 2020. https://www.ohchr.org/EN/NewsEvents/Pages/DisplayNews.aspx?NewsID=26491&LangID=E.
8. Amanda Randone. 'I Became A Free Woman': Leïla Slimani On Leaving Social Media. *Vogue*, 7 November 2020. https://www.vogue.co.uk/arts-and-lifestyle/article/leila-slimani-on-leaving-social media.
9. Elaine Showalter. Killing the Angel in the House: The Autonomy of Women Writers. *The Antioch Review*, vol. 50, no. 1/2, 50th Anniversary Issue (Winter–Spring, 1992), pp. 207–20.

10. Ibid.
11. Ibid.
12. John Berger, *Ways of Seeing* (Penguin, 1972).
13. Mary Shelley, *Frankenstein* (Penguin, 2003).
14. 'The beginning is always today' is widely attributed to Mary Shelley and sometimes her mother, Mary Wollstonecraft. Despite checking both their work, I cannot confirm the origins of the phrase and can only suppose that its spirit is one both Marys, as visionaries for change, would support.

Interviews in order of appearance (some names have been changed)

1. Aubrey, telephone conversation with author, 28 January 2021.
2. Ciara, email exchange with author, 11–23 April 2019.
3. Carolina, Skype conversation with author, 11 September 2020.
4. Jennifer, email exchange with author, 10–16 September 2020.
5. Christina, email exchange with author, 8–16 September 2020.
6. Natalie, email exchange with author, 19–30 September 2020.
7. Verity, email exchange with author, 8–16 September 2020.
8. Jacqueline, telephone conversation with author, 9 September 2020.
9. Pixie, Skype conversation with author, 31 August 2020.
10. Adele, telephone conversation with author, 15 November 2020.
11. Seyi, Skype conversation with author, 23 November 2020.
12. Annmarie, email exchange with author, 6–10 August 2015.
13. Kate, telephone conversation with author, 12 January 2021.
14. Harriet, email exchange with author, 9–14 October 2020.
15. Eve, telephone conversation with author, 12 October 2021.
16. Megan, telephone conversation with author, 12 October 2021 and 28 January 2021.

17. Yuna, telephone conversation with author, 2 November 2020.
18. Phoebe, Skype conversation with author, 8 May 2019.
19. Jane, Skype conversation with author, 5 June 2019.
20. Clare, email exchange with author, 27 Oct–2 Nov 2020.
21. Emma, email exchange with author, 27 Oct–2 Nov 2020.
22. Nighat, text exchange with author, 4–11 November 2020.

Further reading and viewing

Crystal Abidin, *Internet Celebrity: Understanding Fame Online* (Emerald Publishing, 2018); Sarah Banet-Weiser, *Authentic™: The Politics of Ambivalence in a Brand Culture* (NYU Press, 2012); Adam Curtis, *The Century of the Self* (2002 documentary series available on YouTube); Rachel E. Dubrofsky and Shoshana Amielle Magnet (eds), *Feminist Surveillance Studies* (Duke University Press, 2015); Mark Fisher, *Capitalist Realism: Is There No Alternative?* (Zero Books, 2009); Joanne McNeil, *Lurking: How a Person Became a User* (Farrar, Straus and Giroux, 2020); Evgeny Morozov, *The Net Delusion: How Not to Liberate the World* (Penguin, 2011); Jenny Odell, *How to Do Nothing: Resisting the Attention Economy* (Melville House, 2019); Arlie Russell Hochschild, *The Managed Heart: Commercialization of Human Feeling* (University of California Press, 2012); Henry Jenkins, *Convergence Culture: Where Old and New Media Collide* (New York University Press, 2008); Ciarán McMahon, *The Psychology of Social Media* (Routledge, 2019); Leigh Stein, *Self-Care* (Penguin, 2020); Nancy Thumin, *Self-Representation and Digital Culture* (Palgrave Macmillan, 2012); Daniel Trottier, *Social Media as Surveillance: Rethinking Visibility in a Converging World* (Routledge, 2012); Emily van der Meulen and Robert Heynen (eds), *Gender and the Politics of Surveillance* (University of Toronto Press, 2016); José van Dijck, *The Culture of Connectivity:*

A Critical History of Social Media (Oxford University Press, 2013); Sylvie Weil, *Selfies* (translated by Ros Schwartz; Les Fugitives, 2019); James Williams, *Stand Out of Our Light* (YouTube, 2017); Shoshana Zuboff, *The Age of Surveillance Capitalism: The Fight for a Human Future at the New Frontier of Power* (Profile Books, 2019).

Index

Acknowledgements

No human is an island and no book was ever written without the support of a small but vital village. Thank you to my family and friends, and all my colleagues in academia. Huge thanks to my agent, Ivan Mulcahy, and everyone at MMBcreative, especially Sallyanne and Tilly. A special mention for the brilliant team at New Island and commissioning editor extraordinaire Aoife K. Walsh who has been a champion of *TVT* from the outset. To my editor, the wise and wonderful Djinn von Noorden – thank you for all your enthusiasm and attention to detail. And to my cover designer, Jack Smyth, who did such a brilliant job. Thanks also to the very kind Louise O'Neill for her early support. Lastly but by no means least, love to Elmo and Lily, and to G – thank you for being my home.